Come as You're Not

Because God Welcomes You as You Are

*an inspirational message
of hope and overcoming*

BY MICAH ANN DUCKETT

WESTBOW PRESS®
A DIVISION OF THOMAS NELSON
& ZONDERVAN

Copyright © 2017 Micah Ann Duckett.

All rights reserved. No part of this book may be used or reproduced by any means, graphic, electronic, or mechanical, including photocopying, recording, taping or by any information storage retrieval system without the written permission of the author except in the case of brief quotations embodied in critical articles and reviews.

Scriptures marked ASV are taken from the American Standard Version (ASV): American Standard Version, public domain.

Scripture taken from the King James Version of the Bible.

"Scripture taken from the NEW AMERICAN STANDARD BIBLE®, Copyright © 1960,1962,1963,1968,1971,1972,1973,1975,19 77, 1995 by The Lockman Foundation. Used by permission."

THE HOLY BIBLE, NEW INTERNATIONAL VERSION®, NIV® Copyright © 1973, 1978, 1984, 2011 by Biblica, Inc.® Used by permission. All rights reserved worldwide.

This book is a work of non-fiction. Unless otherwise noted, the author and the publisher make no explicit guarantees as to the accuracy of the information contained in this book and in some cases, names of people and places have been altered to protect their privacy.

WestBow Press books may be ordered through booksellers or by contacting:

WestBow Press
A Division of Thomas Nelson & Zondervan
1663 Liberty Drive
Bloomington, IN 47403
www.westbowpress.com
1 (866) 928-1240

Because of the dynamic nature of the Internet, any web addresses or links contained in this book may have changed since publication and may no longer be valid. The views expressed in this work are solely those of the author and do not necessarily reflect the views of the publisher, and the publisher hereby disclaims any responsibility for them.

Any people depicted in stock imagery provided by Thinkstock are models, and such images are being used for illustrative purposes only. Certain stock imagery © Thinkstock.

ISBN: 978-1-5127-8233-2 (sc)
ISBN: 978-1-5127-8235-6 (hc)
ISBN: 978-1-5127-8234-9 (e)

Library of Congress Control Number: 2017905261

Print information available on the last page.

WestBow Press rev. date: 04/17/2017

Dedication

I dedicate this culmination of my journey to God, Who gave me the honor of a front row seat at His display of power, provision and purpose in my life; and to my late mother, Robbie Fern Bell Ksionda, who taught by example that God rewards the patience and faith of a praying woman whose heart is His.

Contents

Introduction ix

Chapter 1   Not Prepared 1
Chapter 2   Not with the Perfect Ending 9
Chapter 3   Not Like I Imagined 17
Chapter 4   Not Knowing What Will Happen 25
Chapter 5   Not What I Wanted 31
Chapter 6   Not Getting It Right 39
Chapter 7   Not Accepted 47
Chapter 8   Not Strong Enough 59
Chapter 9   Not in a Good Place 67
Chapter 10 Not Feeling God's Love 75
Chapter 11 Not Able to Let It Go 83
Chapter 12 Not Recognizing God's Voice 95

Epilogue: Not Alone 105
Reader's Guide for Group Discussion or Self Study ... 115
Study Notes and Journal 125

Introduction

Come as you're not, a personal invitation to allow God to speak through these pages to refresh,

>restore,

>renew,

>regain,

>replenish,

>reinvigorate,

>and refuel.

Remove any facade of pretense and slip into the honesty of the raw, unfiltered truth of all the "not" experiences of being human. Expectantly come as you're not because God welcomes you as you are.

To enhance your reading experience, spend time with God in thought and prayer at the close of a chapter or two. May the communion be pointedly personal and universally uplifting as the union of written text, God's impressions, worship of the heart, and cries of the soul intersect. The message may be personal to you, someone you know, or one you have yet to encounter, who will need a meaningful word or two from this book. Come see what God shows you and hear His encouragement through all the have, am, and are not examples of His overcoming power in my own life.

> *All those the Father gives me will come to me, and whoever comes to me I will never drive away. (John 6:37 NIV)*

Not Prepared

CHAPTER ONE

"Is that Derek's birthday bike?" The mangled, crushed heap held enough of its parts to let me know it was a bicycle, and it drew my attention to the left side of the road in the distance before I slowed in passing to get a better look from my car. A good thing it did because if only I had looked to the right, I would have seen the ambulance and a small group gathered—and probably crashed my vehicle.

It was Saturday, June 2, 1990, Derek's ninth birthday and our seventeenth wedding anniversary. My husband, Mike, would return later that day from out-of-town business, and we would celebrate Derek's birthday. Before Mike left, we had given Derek his new bicycle early, and since that day, the street in front of our home had felt the treads of his numerous laps in fine racing style.

Because of last-minute RSVPs, I needed to make a run to the store for more goodie bag items. Derek begged out of the trip and pleaded to stay instead with his good friend in order to ride bikes together. After checking with the mom and getting the okay, I walked Derek with his new bike to the major intersection at Loop 197 North that separated our neighborhood from his friend's, and I made sure he crossed safely, as was my custom because of the heavy traffic. The boy's home was only a block or so from the intersection, and soon I was off on my party mission.

I cannot explain how I missed something as large as an ambulance with lights upon my return from the store. I believe God drew my attention to what looked like the twisted frame of Derek's new birthday bike. It had not been in our possession long, and a part of me held out hope it was not Derek's bike. The other part of me knew it might be but would not allow me to ask, "Has Derek been hit by a car?" All I could question over and over like a looped statement was, "Is that Derek's birthday bike?"

Somehow, I managed to pull over into the entrance of our subdivision, and as I stepped out of the car, I noticed Ray, my neighbor and church friend, walking with determined pace toward me, face concentrating on the ground, not making eye contact. "Ray! Ray, is that Derek's birthday bike?" I called as if Ray knew that Derek had even received a bike for his birthday, much less what it looked like. Still, I could not ask if Derek had been hurt. "Ray, is that Derek's new birthday bike?"

Ray simply kept walking, hastening his steps, and as he got within arm's reach, his eyes met mine in answer to my repeated question. "Yes, it's Derek's bike." My legs gave way as I gasped in short, panting breaths, and I collapsed into Ray's arms. He gently turned me, and suddenly the ambulance and lights loomed before me. "Why hadn't I seen that?" A small group of people gathered and through the gaps between their legs and feet, I saw a pair of little feet in tennis shoes lying limp to the right and left. "Derek..."

As Ray led me toward the scene, he explained that Derek had grown impatient waiting on my return from the store and asked the friend's mom if he could ride to the house to check and see if I was home yet. She quizzed, "Does your mother let you cross that intersection alone?" and Derek lied and told her I did. Derek managed to cross safely going home and was on his way back to his friend's house when the mother heard the crash and her heart sank in dreaded intuition. A twenty-one-year-old young man had struck Derek with his car, which sent the bike under the car to its destruction and Derek lifted up into the windshield and then thrown off, skidding and flopping like a rag doll down the pavement.

We arrived at the group, and as it parted to let me through, I heard whispers, "That's his mother." Staring in disbelief, the first thing I noticed was Derek's platinum-blond hair dampened and resting against his still head; his body unmoving as he lay on his back. His eyes were shut, and he seemed unconscious, which made me wonder if his brain would function normally again. I glanced at gaping, deep slashes in his legs and arms, long slices exposing the flesh that should be hidden from view. I knelt beside the paramedics working on Derek, who lay deathly still without flinching as they assessed him. "Mama's here, Derek; Mama's here." I was shocked when his head slowly turned toward me in recognition, his eyes searching to find my face.

"Mama."

"Yes, baby, Mama's right here."

Eyes now locked, he pleaded, "Pleeease tell them I don't need stitches!"

"Oh, my God, your brain is still in there and working fine," I breathed in relief as I moved from fighting back tears to embracing chuckles and thanking the Lord. "Sweetheart, we have no choice but to give you a few stitches."

"Well, then, will you tell me how many stitches I get? I want to see if I beat Kyle." Yes, until that fateful day, brother Kyle held the family record for stitches from a couple of minor childhood accidents. Little did we know, not only would Derek assume the family record, it would take over 300 stitches to put him back together. Amazingly, there were no broken bones or internal injuries.

I'm not sure how fast Mike drove home, but his way was cleared thanks to some calls from the chief of police, a personal family friend. He arrived at the hospital just in time to see Derek before they took him to the operating room. While awaiting an update, I prayed, "God, what in the world will I tell Derek when he comes to? Where were Your angels who were supposed to guard Derek? I know he is going to ask me why this had to happen to him, and quite frankly, God, I need an answer to that myself."

I sensed God telling me to read Psalm 91. Don't ask me how I had a Bible in my hands that day. I cannot tell you, but there was my Bible. I began to read,

> *He who dwells in the shelter of the Most High will abide in the shadow of the Almighty. I will say to the LORD, "My refuge and my fortress, My God, in whom I trust!" For it is He who delivers you from the snare of the trapper and from the deadly pestilence. He will cover you with His pinions, and under His wings you may seek refuge; His faithfulness is a shield and bulwark. You will not be afraid of the terror by night, or of the arrow that flies by day; of the pestilence that stalks in darkness, or of the destruction that lays waste at noon. A thousand may fall at your side and ten thousand at your right hand, but it shall not approach you. You will only look on with your eyes and see the recompense of the wicked. For you have made the LORD, my refuge, even the Most High, your dwelling place. No evil will befall you, nor will any plague come near your tent. For He will give His angels charge concerning you, to guard you in all your ways. They will bear you up in their hands, that you do not strike your foot against a stone. (Psalm 91:1–12 NASB)*

I sensed God interrupting me, "Stop. Go back and read verses 11–12: 'For He will give His angels charge concerning you, to guard you in all your ways. They will bear you up in their hands, that you do not strike your foot against a stone.' Personalize those verses. Remember what the policeman said at the scene?"

I did remember the officer telling me that Derek should have been dragged under the car with the bike, mangled, and killed. Somehow, he was lifted up and thrown into the windshield. I personalized the verses: "For God gave His angels charge concerning Derek, to guard him in all his ways. They bore Derek up in their hands and into the windshield, lest he be dragged under the car and killed."

I had my answer, and when Derek woke, he certainly did ask me why this happened to him. I was able to explain that God had saved his life, as I read the verses and personalized them for him. The words quieted his spirit and seemed to bring some relief.

Interestingly, years later as a young man in the United States Marine Corps, Derek called me one day to read a cool psalm that a buddy of his had shown him. As Derek read the words of Psalm 91, I immediately recognized them, and when he finished reading, I reminded Derek why that psalm spoke to him. Suddenly he remembered, and for a brief moment the thought flittered in my mind and out of my mouth, "I wonder why God is reminding us of that psalm?" This happened two weeks before 9/11, and when that terrible day arrived, my fleeting question came flooding back like a tsunami in full awareness, for I knew that incident could not go unanswered by the United States of America. It brought to mind that should we go to war and Derek be deployed, my son was in God's sovereign care, whether Derek lived or died, because God recorded the number of his days in a book before Derek was conceived according to Psalm 139:16.

I am well aware that life hands us things for which we are not prepared, and they don't all have perfect endings. Why should angels save my child and not another mother's child just as deserving? Why should Psalm 91:11–12 "work" for me and not someone else? Is my family more deserving of mercy than yours? We will explore those questions in the next chapter.

For this day, let me close with this for your contemplation. We will not always be prepared when devastating things happen, but we can have an emergency response at the ready. Mine has always been to look to the Lord with bold faith. Scripture says it best in Hebrews 4:16 NASB: "Therefore let us draw near with confidence to the throne of grace, so that we may receive mercy and find grace to help in time of need."

If these words find you caught off guard by some emergency circumstance or crushing setback, come not prepared and discover the mercy and grace which have been readied for such a time as this.

Not with the Perfect Ending

CHAPTER TWO

Wouldn't it be wonderful if life's struggles ultimately end with "happily ever after?" Warring countries become great allies. Devastating illness is healed by a miracle or a newfound cure. Mommies and Daddies stay happily in love, and children know nothing of abuse, abandonment, or anger. Justice works fairly for all skin colors and people get what they deserve. The most qualified person is hired, and everyone has a job that pays the bills and provides for some charitable donations, leisure activities and vacations. Doors have no locks because everyone respects your space. Street drugs were never invented, and no one wants to blow up your country.

As much as we would love nothing more than to live happily ever after, we cannot change the fact that sin, sickness, death and evil exist in our fallen world. We are fallen beings existing in bodies prone and susceptible to sin, disease and illness. Bad things happen to good people, and bad things happen to bad people. Good things happen to bad people, and good things happen to good people. Good and bad things happen according to how we define those terms. For instance, rain on the day of an outdoor wedding is not good or welcomed, but rain in a drought-stricken land is both welcomed and good. I do know this from James 1:17, however, that every good and perfect gift is from above, coming down from the Father of the heavenly lights, who does not change like shifting shadows.

We need to remember that last phrase about God, "who does not change like shifting shadows," because we are met with obstacles that can challenge our perspective of God's love for us. We have a tendency to rate the quality of God's care and concern on the outcome of a crisis as we perceive what is "perfect." *The outcome of a situation, good or bad, is not the measure of our Savior's love and care for us.* God's unmatched, unmerited love for each human being has never shifted or flickered for a moment. It traces back to a time before creation when the plan to rescue man from hell was devised. The Bible puts it like this:

> *Since you call on a Father who judges each person's work impartially, live out your time as foreigners here in reverent fear. For you know that it was not with perishable things such as silver or gold that you were redeemed from the empty way of life handed down to you from your ancestors, but with the precious blood of Christ, a lamb without blemish or defect. He was chosen* **before the creation of the world***, but was revealed in these last times for your sake.* (I Peter 1:17–20 NIV)

Remember, God did not create a rescue plan for the angels that fell from heaven. They are doomed to hell. However, God loved mankind with an everlasting love and did not want anyone to perish, yet He desired to give man a free will to make his own choices. Before the first word was spoken into creation, a plan was made to eternally save man from everything from a simple lapse in judgment, to things brought on through no fault of man's own, to all-out rebellion and rejection. God and Jesus saw the best and worst in each person, and Jesus, the key to making this work, was both able and willing to lay down His life as a spotless lamb in ransom of all people for all time.

| Come as You're Not |

Together the Father and Son went forward with the salvation plan at great cost and to this day offer the opportunity to anyone to become a part of His family through Jesus Christ.

When the tough times come, we have to remind ourselves of this merciful love because it can look like we've been abandoned, unheard, rejected and/or unloved by God. When a little child or loved one is involved and there is no cure or relief on the horizon, it can appear that God must surely be cold and heartless. When you are a parent of a toddler who is writhing in pain for days from a hospital bed, it is an understandable response to wonder how God can hear this and do nothing to intercede.

There is no magic formula to guarantee our stories end well by our standards, but we can choose how we will manage them. I am not saying this is easy. In fact, it can be agonizing as we come to grips with the new reality thrown at us. My definition of a best outcome looks different from what I get at times. It is impossible to find "because answers" that make sense of the "why questions" I posed in chapter one. *There are mysteries not meant to be solved, but God's sovereignty is there to be found.* I may not discern answers to all my questions, God's logic may be unattainable by my finite mind, and the silence from heaven may seem deafening, but I can rule out the answers that say God does not care, He is cruel and heartless, and God is not love. When I am tempted to get angry with God for not intervening or to slip into abandonment's tug at my heart, I remind myself that Calvary proved God's love. I can trust God's heart for me and my loved ones and stand surefooted on the Rock of that hill where "love ran red" for us, as Chris Tomlin pens it.

I know what it is like not to have the perfect ending. My family was vacationing when we received word one morning that a loved one had passed away unexpectedly under suspicious circumstances, not natural causes. As the days unfolded, we were forced to see the ugly realities of my loved one's private life, but it was too late to help. Instead, we had information overload that we could hardly wrap our minds around. Shocking "TMI" bombarded us at once, making our shields of faith feel like they were taking on armor-piercing bullets.

Approximately eleven months prior to this tragedy, I made a trip to see this person one night following an outdoor religious crusade. During the sermon, I sensed that I needed to go talk to this loved one about getting right with God, and it could not wait. I had to go that night, and I did. Upon my arrival, I explained my urgent prompting to deliver this message from God which seemed so urgent that it could not even wait until morning, but the message was rejected with the added comment that although not ready at the moment to take this path, my loved one promised to get back in touch with God someday. I felt prompted to say words that would prove prophetic: "Well, when you're ready, it may be too late."

On the drive home, I second-guessed myself for saying it may be too late. I never dreamed this person would be dead within the year. Plus I knew it is never too late for God to accept you with all that you're not and then transform your life into so much more than you are, could hope, or imagine when you submit to Him. Suddenly it was eleven months later, and those words came rushing back to me during this nightmare. I understood why God had prompted me to deliver that warning. It might be too late, not because God would ever reject a person's return to Him, but because no one knows what a day holds. You might not be alive and in a position to make that change. You have some control over your own life but not over your circumstances or the lives of other people every minute of the day. Life is constantly changing and full of surprises, some of them not so good.

No family is immune from tragedy because sin, death, sickness, and evil were introduced into our world in the Garden of Eden. God never promised us a life without trials. To the contrary, Jesus said in John 16:33 NASB, "These things I have spoken to you, so that in Me you may have peace. In the world you have tribulation, but take courage; I have overcome the world." When I became a Christ follower and surrendered my life to take on His, Jesus imparted this same overcoming power in me. It is why I can find courage to persevere through the worst trials.

I know God cared about my loved one and He sent a warning through me, but He was also a God of His Word. He promised to give a free will, and He followed through to allow the choice to meet its end. When I was too devastated to hold anything, I came without my perfect ending and found that my Rock of Salvation and Anchor of my Soul held me. Come without your perfect ending, and give God time to write the rest of your story.

Not Like I Imagined

CHAPTER THREE

Many times things don't turn out like we imagined, and often the outcome is not good. Children rebel, loved ones die, spouses cheat, finances change, accidents happen, friends fade, people betray, jobs disappear, health fails, dreams disintegrate, and crimes crush. We may find "why answers" here on earth or we may have to wait till eternity when everything is revealed.

There were moments in my childhood when life was not like I imagined. Before God changed my father's heart, he was prone to a terrible temper that could erupt suddenly, sometimes evoking rage and abuse. I lived in terror of those moments. Other times, there was no rage or a hint of a temper flare-up; he would walk over and slap me without warning because he did not like the expression on my face. Living under these circumstances caused me to constantly think through every detail of any action I took to make sure I did not do anything to set him off. In my childlike mind, I thought I could control my circumstances by making things perfect and doing everything to perfection, which in turn might keep Daddy from "being mean" to me. This is where I began to learn the erroneous lesson of taking the blame and responsibility for someone else's bad behavior; the "it's my fault" lesson.

On the plus side, I grew up to become an adult who is a

great asset as an employee or as a member of a planning team because I will think of every detail that needs to be done and see it through to perfection. On the negative side, I can drive my poor husband nuts, for instance, with some of the house and party preparations to entertain guests, details which most do not notice or care about, honestly. I am a work in progress, and I do understand why those tendencies are ingrained in me. Today I put them to good use when needed and try to rein them in where applicable.

First grade was not as I imagined either. I had so looked forward to going to school and getting out of my home. From the first day, my teacher put me in a closet; not every day thereafter but often. I can still feel her tight grip around my wrist and the tug of my body trying to keep up with that teacher's determined pace. Can you envision a child leaving one environment, expecting an escape, only to discover the teacher seemed to like everyone in the class but you? Can you imagine what this does to a child's self-esteem? I did not understand what I did to make her put me in the closet. I still have no clue what she was thinking, but as I sat in the dark closet, that habit reared its head of assuming the blame for someone else's poor behavior.

In those days when you got in trouble at school, you got in trouble again at home before any questions were asked for your side of the story. Therefore, I was terrified about Daddy finding out that I was so bad at school, my teacher had to put me in the closet for punishment, and I would not be able to answer why. I never mentioned it and he never brought it up. It did not take long for me to realize the teacher was not reporting it to my parents, so sitting in that closet and not telling anyone about it was just fine with me to make sure Daddy never found out. Not once did I complain. In fact, I was an adult before I told

Mom about it one day after I had spent time trying to recall what I could have done to make that teacher not like me. As I searched my memory with an adult's honest, critical eye, it occurred to me that because I was so terrified of what could happen at home if a teacher reported me for bad behavior, I never would have done anything in class to cause me to get in trouble at school. It was my "proof" of sorts for myself that allowed me to finally broach the concept that I was innocent and the teacher was the guilty party. Thus began the process of healing and learning that things were not as I imagined, and in this case that was a good thing because it is not always my fault. Sometimes when things are not like we imagined, it is because our vantage point is skewed, and we need a more informed perspective.

I remember praying for my dad with my mom all those years as she chose to stay in the home. She did not pray for an escape or the means to leave. She prayed for God to change my dad's heart and for our strength to endure until that happened. As a child, I interpreted this to mean we were praying for a miracle because I did not know how a change was going to happen. I could not imagine it.

I am not saying that everyone in an abusive situation should take this stay-put approach because only God and you know if He would want you to leave for a time, stay a bit longer, or leave forever. For Mama, staying long enough to give God time to work was what she felt like God wanted her to do. She had such a beautiful soul, long-suffering patience, and abiding faith in God. She taught me the power of prayer because one day I saw the rage switch turn off in my dad. He still had a short temper and yelled, but his outbursts of rage and violent behavior disappeared as he became a new creation in Christ. We prayed for a miracle in Daddy's heart, and God allowed me to see that come to fruition as I forgave him. Dad and I were able to have a loving, close relationship and create many happy memories to replace the bad ones before he passed away decades later. The cycle of abuse ended with his death.

Sometimes things are not as we imagined because we are expecting a different outcome. As an adult, there was one time in my life when I was the one who needed God to do a miracle in my own mind and spirit, to change me to align my heart to His will, because God's outcome was not the blessing I imagined, expected and anticipated. The power to impact many lives and possibly lose relationships teetered on the precipice of my response to this result that followed much prayer. I knew it was not God's will for me to hold bitterness, stoke disappointment and nurse festering wounds, but I was crushed and unable to get over it. I found myself facing the challenge to prove what I truly believed about picking up my cross and following Jesus. *It is one thing to say you believe something, but it is another to put your money where your mouth is and DO it.* Would I truly align my will to accept His *and sincerely believe it to be the best outcome*, even when I did not understand, have all the answers, or feel good about it yet? I had to pray something like this:

> *Lord, You know this outcome is devastating to me and not like I imagined. At the same time, I know how You would have me respond, but no matter how desperately I WANT to obey, I simply don't know that I can. This is too big for me to just 'get over.' Search my heart. You know I speak the truth. If this outcome that I did not expect is truly Your will for whatever reason, You know that this is more than I can handle. I absolutely cannot do it even though my heart wants to be obedient. I really mean that, but it is impossible. What am I to do? You ask too much of me. If I am going to be able to move forward in obedience with relationships intact, the only*

response I can conceive is You will need to perform a miracle in my heart to equip me to bear it and accept it with no ill feelings. If You do that, then I am willing to wait until I get to heaven for You to explain to me why things turned out as they did. I promise to trust You in the wake of this troubling turn of events. This is not what I imagined would happen today, but I do believe You will do what is best for all concerned. I trust that You will not reject me as I dare to say these words to You, even though all I have to offer is a willing spirit in return for You to change me to accept the outcome of this day. My heart and my will are laid out as an offering before You as a step of faith before I see the miracle. What will You do with me?

Did you catch the key? I had a willing spirit that acted in faith. You may have heard the latter part of Matthew 26:41 quoted from time to time, "…The spirit is willing but the flesh is weak." My spirit was willing but my flesh was impossible to bring into alignment. I had to come to God with nothing to offer but a willing heart. He did not fail to answer that invitation. I call it doing a miracle in my heart because I felt so totally opposite of where I needed to be that it would take a miracle to change me. Guess what? I learned that God is the master of miracles of the heart. His response was swift and sure, my burden was lifted, and I do believe the outcome was right because I know God's will is better than any plan or dream I could fathom.

Do you find yourself in a situation not as you imagined, perhaps testing your faith? Was your childhood spent in a home like mine? Maybe you know someone facing this.

Do you know what it is like to be mistreated by a teacher or someone in authority? Could you identify with being crushed when you did not get the outcome you imagined? The best thing that can happen is for God's will to be done, even if the outcome is not what you envisioned, because His will is perfect and His heart is for us. If you don't have much to offer like I did, come as you're not because God proved to you in creation that He has the ability to make something from nothing by the power of His Word. God's outcome may not be as you always imagined, but I guarantee you will discover a path opened to you which allows for a life worth continuing as you move forward with God's help in the midst of your struggle. Take time to come to God with things not as you imagined, and be willing to let God do a miracle in your heart if needed to accept His will for this leg of your journey together.

Not Knowing What Will Happen

CHAPTER FOUR

"The end is near. You need to come." Hard words to hear about your Mom. The year we found out Mom had inoperable colon cancer that had spread to her liver and lungs was the same year Daddy retired in January. Mom and Dad had saved their whole lives for retirement. They did without niceties like a dishwasher and clothes dryer, saving every penny so they could buy an Airstream Travel Trailer to vacation for weeks when he retired. They had never camped, but this was a lifelong dream about to come true.

On their virgin voyage to Colorado and Canada in July of that year with some veteran campers caravanning together, they didn't even make it out of their home state of Texas before they had to turn back. Mom had a terrible cough, low-grade fever, and felt awful. I helped Daddy get Mom to the doctor upon their return, and after an extensive exam and testing, Daddy sent me home with her while he waited to receive a prescription for cough medicine to fill at the local pharmacy. He took a long time returning and when he arrived, I noticed Dad carried no cough medicine. Instead, he ordered me out of the room, but Mama said, "No, we will hear this together," as she reached for my hand from the sofa where she rested. Daddy fell into his chair, planted his face in his hands, and with heaving shoulders sobbed out the words, "It's cancer, not a cold." I joined his weeping without hesitation, but Mama was the strong one. Most of the time she was Mom to me, sometimes Mother, but there were tender times when she was still Mama, even though I was an adult. This was one.

My siblings were notified and at Mom's request we planned one of our traditional family barbecues while we were gathered to share the burden of terrible news. On that day, Mom rested on the sofa enjoying the grandkids when the doorbell rang just as we were bringing the food off the grill about noon. In filed every person from the youngest to the eldest who had attended the Mexican Baptist Mission that morning, where Mom's diagnosis was announced. They decided to go together straight from church to see their friend in her time of need, and they even brought the accordion they used in worship.

My mother had taught adult English reading and writing to them with the aid of an interpreter, and she had helped many of those people earn their citizenship. She joined their mission work and shared their prayer requests, but most of all, Mama simply loved them. It was obvious the feeling was mutual that day, as not a dry eye could be found.

One by one they approached the sofa to hug and kiss her, pray over her, and share private words of love and encouragement. Then the pastor of that mission anointed Mother's head with oil and prayed for her. Soon the accordion started up, and they began to sing in Spanish. I did not know their words but I knew the song immediately, "Amazing Grace." Our voices in English joined theirs in Spanish, and I could not help but feel like I was getting a glimpse of heaven. The outpouring of love was so tender and genuine that my tears found release as I paused my singing to pray:

> *Lord, is this how people from every tribe and tongue will be able to communicate in heaven? Will we recognize the tune and use our native tongues to sing the words but still understand each other? Perhaps we will communicate because we will know a whole new song with its own language.*

When that call came in early October for me to come, I was a young mother with three children. We did not live in the same town, and to be at the hospital for an unknown amount of time meant a motel room and money for gasoline and food. My husband and I struggled financially at that time, and we did not have the money for this need. I had already made several trips to see her in those final months, but of course, I wanted to be right by her side at the end. My husband and I decided to trust God with our financial needs and believe that somehow, He would provide the money to cover this trip, even if I ended up staying a week in a motel room. Only God knew our concerns. As it turned out, I only needed that room for a couple of nights. She died October 5th.

Shortly after I returned from the funeral, I received a letter with no return address, and the postmark was so light I could not make out the name of the city, if it was there at all. The letter was hand addressed in beautiful calligraphy. The first thing I noticed upon opening the envelope was a wad of cash. An unsigned note with that same impressive handwriting accompanied it, "God told me to send this to you." I counted out $251. "That's an odd amount," I mused, but then my heart leaped, "I wonder...." I gathered my receipts for the motel room, gasoline, and food to total: two hundred fifty dollars and some odd cents. Basically $251 - exactly what I needed. To this day, I have no idea who sent me that money.

Can you imagine being the person who sent it? You sense God is telling you a certain young couple could probably use some money. "How much, God? $251? Okay, I'll send them $250. What? It needs to be $251? Why? I don't get it. Won't they think this odd amount is weird? Okay, okay. $251 it is." At least, this is how I imagine the conversation went. There was no denying God's hand at work and someone's obedience to respond exactly as instructed.

I'm not trying to tell you that every time I had a need in my life, God responded immediately in such a dramatic way. Sometimes there was a delay that did not allay our worries one bit. Other times the need remained but somehow, He brought us through it. Then there were those times when the response was so fast I was amazed.

What about your needs today? What are the needs of your friends and family? Have you cried out to God, but heaven reverberated with silence? Don't back down. Pray with persistence, perseverance, and patience. Your help *is* on the way. Come not knowing what will happen, and rest in His arms at the ready to receive your burdens.

> *There in the twists and turns and ebb and flow of survival, we discover the mettle of God's character and care.*
> — Micah Duckett

Humble yourselves, therefore, under God's mighty hand, that he may lift you up in due time. Cast all your anxiety on Him because He cares for you. (I Peter 5:6–7 NIV)

Not What I Wanted

CHAPTER FIVE

A better chapter title is "Not What I Wanted Then, Not What I Want Now, Not Ever, Ever, Ever!" Yeah, that title is a bit too long, but it gives a better clue about this chapter. I will never forget the day vanity changed my life forever, as it forced me into a new normal. It wasn't your typical idea of vanity, but I have to be honest with myself, and that is the ugly truth.

I was on my way to a Christian women's conference in Austin, Texas, to teach a seminar about overcoming entitled, "So I've Made the Lemonade and I've Still Got Lemons." Many times, I would serve as a musician at conferences and retreats, and other times I would do double duty as a speaker and musician. A dear friend, Chris, often traveled with me so I would not have to travel alone, plus we always had a great time and learned much from the various speakers when I did not have responsibilities of my own. Usually I pulled in her driveway and honked the horn to let her know I was there for pickup. This is where vanity crept in on that fateful day. "I think I will go ring her doorbell today instead of honking the horn. It's really a little classier to do that. I won't go in. I'll just ring the bell and come back to the car to wait." That decision changed my life forever, but I would not know it for a few months.

I knew Chris owned an aggressive Chow, so I had no plan to put my hand on the doorknob, much less open it and walk into her home unannounced. As I started up the sidewalk, I did not realize Chris' interior front door was standing open with the outer glass storm door pulled shut because her storm door was tinted. I could not see through it; the dog, however, saw me through that tint and started charging the storm door. Just as I reached the porch and my finger was heading toward the doorbell, the dog's charge was perfectly timed so that he leaped and hit the door hard enough to break through the glass. One second I was about to ring the doorbell and in the next split second, a snarling dog was in midair flying at my face, teeth bared.

I was able to react quickly enough to use two hands to shove the dog in the neck and shoulder area with a left to right motion, forcing his head away from my face. At the same time, my reaction caused me to jerk my head and upper torso away from his face and fall to the ground on my back. The next thing I knew, the dog had latched onto my left leg like a vise, shaking his head and growling much like a pup with a pull toy. I was able to come to a seated position to slip my fingers into a small gap between my leg and his top teeth, trying to lift up to keep him from biting down so hard. All the while I was screaming for Chris, and I guess the intensity of need was clear in my screams because the doors of neighbor houses flew open and people came running. Chris made it outside, and all I could say was, "Oh, Chris; oh, Chris," as she managed to pull the dog off me and into the house.

After an ambulance ride and a few stitches at the local hospital, Chris and I headed to the conference, having notified them why I would arrive a bit late. My poor friend had to hear me tell the story over and over throughout the weekend as people asked me about it. I was sad this had happened to me, but I was more concerned about Chris because I could imagine how I would feel in a role reversal where my dog attacked Chris without provocation. Her dog had to be quarantined, and because this was the second time he had bitten someone unprovoked, the dog had to be put down. You can imagine how hard this was for Chris. It was a terrible accident and I knew she felt awful about it, but naturally this pierced her heart because her pet was a family member. Both of us were thankful the person on the porch that day was not a child going door-to-door for a school fundraiser because the outcome could have been much worse. Through it all, however, neither of us would let this incident come between our friendship.

A couple of months passed, and I noticed that my energy level had really dropped off. I was the person people would describe by saying, "I don't know how she does everything," but now I found myself struggling to keep up. I chalked it up to aging and pushed forward. Then I noticed my legs and feet were swelling as my weakness, pain and fatigue grew worse. My legs would throb worse when I was in a seated position with my feet on the floor. Elevating my legs seemed to help, so I was spending more time in my recliner at home. It was becoming more difficult to work a full day at my desk job because of the swelling and pain.

One night my husband noticed my toenails turning a light purple and he suggested I consult a doctor. After a few doctor visits and several tests, I was referred to a podiatrist, who diagnosed me with lymphedema in both legs and feet. The diagnosis was confirmed by other doctors I consulted for second and third opinions. There is no cure for lymphedema, which is caused by trauma to the lymphatic system, and in my case, the trauma was the dog attack, as the bite was deep enough to cause damage. It confused me because the dog only bit me on my left leg, but I soon learned that indeed others had contracted lymphedema in both limbs following a dog attack on one limb. Although I had never heard of this, I found out it was not rare. The doctors served as expert witnesses in court cases on this issue.

This condition is not life threatening but it is definitely life altering. Because the lymphatic system has a connection to the immune system, my immune system is compromised as well. It takes a long time for me to recover from illness and injuries. A simple scratch can take weeks to heal, so you can imagine how devastating it could be if I were to contract something like West Nile virus. In fact, my doctor encouraged me to try not to get a mosquito bite because of what they carry and how that could have a poor outcome with me.

There are three stages of lymphedema, and while there is no cure for it, I can prevent it from advancing to the next stage. Although I am disabled, I remain in stage one today with diligence to do several things to manage my condition. For instance, to help control the swelling, I wear custom compression garments, but even with that, because of the swelling, I can no longer wear heels of any size for any amount of time nor closed-toe shoes for very long. Good-bye, cute shoes. I can hear the collective sigh of many kindred hearts on that one!

I went from being the woman that made people wonder how she did it all to the person who has difficulty making it through the day. I went from athletic and slim to requiring a cane to get around and packing on weight. Many of my activities came to a screeching halt, and I am unable to stand for longer than 10-15 minutes or walk any distance. I am unable to participate in some activities with my grandchildren, and by now I trust you get the idea that my life looks quite different from what I pictured it would at this age.

I did not ask or plan for a dog to attack me or for my body to develop lymphedema from this attack. I did not want my life to change, but it did. How did I handle it and stay positive? I was faced with some choices:

- To be depressed about it, or accept my new normal;
- To blame God for not protecting me, or to investigate how I could still be useful in God's plan that included a big twist I did not see coming;
- To hold a grudge against Chris, or to remain close friends and see this accident as beyond anyone's control.

I chose to look for the positives and prayed something like this:

> *God, please heal me if it fits in Your plans for my life, but if healing me of lymphedema would take me away from Your best for me, then give me eyes to see how I can be useful to You. Teach me lessons from my new normal as You help me come to terms with it.*

That was 2005, and to this day God continues to open ministry doors to me in the strangest places and ways, many of which can be done from a recliner, aka my war room. Do I wish I had honked the horn that day instead of walking to the doorbell? Sure. Is there great purpose to my life in this new normal? Absolutely, and I am fulfilled by a loving God I trust. There are amazing stories of "divine appointments" and ministry opportunities that I would have missed in my busier days. Life hurled me headlong into change, but God held my hand and rolled me right into a new normal.

Can you relate to what it means to come to terms with your

new normal? Have you been able to find your new purpose? Maybe you can relate because you know someone who had to face life with a new normal. Take some time to come to God with what you did not want and let Him inspire you to be all He wants you to be in your new normal.

> *The steps of a man are established by the Lord, and He delights in his way. When he falls, he will not be hurled headlong, because the Lord is the One who holds his hand. (Psalm 37.23–24 NASB)*

Not Getting It Right

CHAPTER SIX

Have you ever thought you were following open doors and signs from God about His will, only to find out you were mistaken? Perhaps you have picked up the pieces and come alongside a friend suffering the fallout of such an error. Maybe your divine appointment on this topic is yet in the future. Here's a look at where my husband and I went wrong with the best of intentions and how God corrected the terrible mess we made.

Mike and I found out we would become second-time parents, and our two-year-old cotton top son, "Dutch," was about to learn he would finally become a big brother. In the midst of parenting joys, our lives were filled with Mike's coaching career and church activities. Life was good and we were dedicated to following God wherever He led. For several years, Mike sensed there was more for him in service to God, especially in the growing area of church activities ministry. The intensity of those feelings grew as God dealt with him about surrendering full-time to that ministry. We kept these thoughts between us, prayed for God's direction, and made ourselves available for anything God showed us as we waited for an open door, a sign, anything to point us in the right direction.

About that time, our then-pastor approached Mike out of the blue about a new direction for the church that he had held confidential until that moment, sharing it with Mike. "I haven't told the deacons or anyone at the church about this yet, but I strongly sense God wants us to build a family life activities center, and I want you to pray about coming on staff as family life minister. First, I need to go to the deacons and then the church to get the building started. Later in the process, I will put your name forward as the man we need to hire if you feel led to do it, but until that time, keep all of this quiet and start praying about your role."

We were stunned and naturally looked at this surprise wrinkle in our plans as confirmation from God because it had fallen in our laps like manna from heaven. No one knew we had already been praying about the activities ministry except God, and then miraculously the pastor basically offered Mike a staff position as family life minister. In the months to follow, there were many private conversations and meetings between the pastor and Mike as the building plans moved along to fruition. It was exciting to watch the plan unfold, and it appeared to sail through door after open door, as the dream was welcomed by the deacons, approved by the church, Mike's private conversations with the pastor continued, and the building took shape. The project neared completion as the school year was ending. Mike needed to let the school and coaching staff know that he would not return the next school year since he would be moving to full-time ministry at the church. Before we could do that, however, it was necessary for Mike to know when his name would be presented to the deacons because we did not want the confidential church news to leak prematurely through Mike's resignation. The days neared the deadline in Mike's secular career for resignations to be submitted, but calls to the pastor were not being returned now for some reason. That should have been a big red flag to us, but over the building months, the pastor often confirmed to us that his vision remained unchanged. While we felt a bit desperate to let the school and coaching staff know something right away at this point, we did not suspect that the pastor's plans for Mike had changed. To add to our growing anxiety, I was at my due date and no gap in insurance coverage was imperative; therefore, the transition needed to happen soon.

While we stressed over this dilemma, the pastor preached a sermon on stepping out in faith and offered illustrations from the Bible about people who acted in faith first and then an activity of God followed. Over lunch Mike and I tossed around the idea that maybe God was testing our faith and perhaps wanted us to move forward with the resignation without telling anyone Mike's plans. We would not break any confidentiality, but it would be a sign of good faith before God like we learned in the sermon. God's activity was surely coming any day now, and we could trust Him to hold off this baby I needed to deliver until the other job and insurance were in place. After a couple more days of praying and getting the word from the pastor to move forward with the resignation, we took the leap of faith.

Word of the resignation spread, and soon thereafter the pastor requested a meeting at our home that night, which ultimately would shatter our innocence and naïveté. When he arrived, he was accompanied by the chairman of the deacons. We did not know anyone else was coming, so when they walked in together, Mike and I were briefly confused but quickly thought it seemed logical to bring him to discuss Mike filling the staff position. That is why they came, right?

Talk about a blindside. The TV program *Survivor* has nothing on our blindside. They came to tell us that after learning more about the qualifications needed to run a family life program and operate the building, the deacons and pastor decided they needed to hire someone with experience. Mike was not their candidate for the job.

While the pastor went on to apologize and accept blame for allowing Mike to quit his job and not telling him right away about the change in direction, I sat there contemplating the harsh reality that I was two weeks overdue with our second child and Mike had no job and no insurance. This baby could come at any time, we had another child to feed already, and now neither of us had a job. After Mike saw them out and shut the door, we both sobbed and realized we had followed a man, rather than God. Our intentions were good, and we thought God was speaking to us through the pastor, but we were sincerely wrong and in deep trouble. We sought the counsel of wiser friends that night, a former pastor and his wife.

In the middle of the mess we had made, God taught us something about His role as a righteous judge. He knew our hearts were earnest and our intentions pure, and God set about showing us that when He looks upon hearts like ours, He transforms the mess into something meaningful. Jeremiah puts it like this:

> *Blessed is the man who trusts in the LORD and whose trust is the LORD, for he will be like a tree planted by the water that extends its roots by a stream and will not fear when the heat comes; but its leaves will be green, and it will not be anxious in a year of drought nor cease to yield fruit. The heart is more deceitful than all else and is desperately sick; who can understand it?* **I, the LORD, search the heart, I test the mind, even to give to each man according to his ways, according to the results of his deeds.** *(Jeremiah 17:7–10 NASB)*

God rescued us with one visit to the head coach, who told Mike to report the next day. He did not know where

Mike would teach and he might have to teach several different subjects, but there would be a place for Mike and our insurance would not be impacted. Shortly thereafter, big brother Dutch welcomed Kyle Brandon, or "Brudder Kowl" as Dutch called him, and our little family weathered the hard lessons.

God taught us some things about His patience as we tried to help God out, much like Abram and Sarai tried to help God give them a child through Hagar (Genesis 16). Since God had promised them an heir but Sarah had not conceived for years, they decided maybe God wanted to give them an heir through her handmaiden. They ran ahead of God and took matters into their own hands. Mike and I ran ahead of God, and like them, we tried to help Him out but made a mess of things instead of getting it right. Just as God sorted out the mess made by Abram and Sarai, He turned our situation around and taught us about His sovereignty.

The latter half of I Samuel 16:7 NASB tells us, "…God sees not as man sees, for man looks at the outward appearance, but the LORD looks at the heart." Spend time alone with God as He looks upon the desires of your heart and hears your need for direction. Come even if you haven't gotten it right and let God show you that transforming messes is one of His specialties.

Not Accepted

CHAPTER SEVEN

Although there are many good and caring people in our churches, some of my deepest wounds have come from church people. It is sad to think that the place which should be the safest is at times the cruelest. Certainly, an action can be unintentional, while other times it is calculated or snarky with an intent to strike a blow. This is not God's plan for His church, and I know it hurts His heart to witness the latter. What I have learned is that God has a way of sending His cavalry to the rescue at precisely the right moment, but to paint the whole picture, let me take you back to the beginning that led me to this lesson.

As far back as I can remember, I loved music and all things musical, especially the piano. In my fifth-grade year, I asked to take piano lessons, but my parents refused with excuses like, "You won't practice. There will be wailing and gnashing of teeth as we force you to practice. We don't have the money, and even if we did, the money would be wasted because you will not stick to it," and similar negative comments.

My sister, Carla, nine years older than I, had taken piano lessons, so not to be thwarted, I proceeded to read from the pages of her beginner piano book every day after school. I looked at the demonstrative drawings, read the text on the page, and began to teach myself to play. I was a strict self-instructor, not allowing myself to move on to the next lesson until I had mastered the current one. At last my parents relented and decided to give me a chance with a piano teacher. It was the greatest gift ever, and I understood that this instrument would not be learned in a few easy lessons. It would take work, but if I put in plenty of effort, then I would master the piano and make music. I practiced so much that my daddy would spank me to make me *stop* practicing the piano! Have you ever heard of such a thing? Neither have I as of this writing, but then, I was always a different child! If this were a text instead of a book, I would insert a smiley face emoji here.

After a couple of years of lessons, I could sight-read most anything set before me, and I had a true passion for this instrument. I was able to take piano lessons from fifth grade to my junior year of high school. I do not want to misrepresent myself here, though. I'm not the next Liberace, nor have I ever desired to be a classically-trained concert pianist as a profession, but there is an undeniable connection between my soul and notes expressed in my playing. It is a talent I believe God gave me. I played for my church throughout my teen years and served as an accompanist at school, theater, competitions, and so forth. In fact, one of the ways I serve God to this day is as pianist at my church with the orchestra; however, it wasn't until my young adult years that I realized God had anointed my playing in a miraculous way.

At age twenty-one in my daily private prayer time one night, I decided I wanted to dedicate my musical talent to God so I prayed something like this:

> *Lord, it is evident to me that You have given me a special talent and passion for playing the piano, and I would like to dedicate my talent to Your glory. If You will use me, I will play for You, and it does*

not matter if I'm playing for a congregation of five thousand people or a Sunday School class of ten people. I don't care if I play perfectly or mess up terribly as long as You are glorified. Well, sure, I want to play well, but I'm not asking You to make me play well. What I mean is, even if I mess up, as long as You are glorified and pleased, then that is the most important thing to me. Please use me for Your glory as You see fit. My answer is yes to any call You send my way.

It was a "here am I; send me" type of prayer. I did not ask for more talent. I did not ask for a specific place to be used. I told no one about my prayer, and I did not think much about it afterwards. The next morning, however, I thought a lot about it because something happened. I sat down to play as I did every day, but this time those runs up the keyboard were effortless---in every key signature. I tried other techniques that had given me a struggle in the days before, but now I found them to be no problem---in every key. By this time, my heart raced at the thought, "*I think God did a miracle in me.*"

Next, I tried playing a hymn arrangement that I had heard in my head the days before but could never find the right combination of notes to create the chords needed to achieve the sound I wanted to use. Suddenly, I simply knew what notes were needed to make those chords, and I began my journey into writing that hymn arrangement while the thoughts lingered, "God definitely did a miracle in me. I wonder what He is up to? I did not ask Him to do all this. I just asked to be used. This is crazy!"

When Mike came home from work, I could not contain the announcement, "God did a miracle in me. Come see!" Mike must have thought for a moment I had lost it as I scurried off to the piano, but that did not last long when I started to play. It was the most amazing thing, and for the first time, I shared with him about my dedication prayer. We kept this to ourselves and waited to see what God would do.

Within three days, I began to receive calls from representatives of different churches who had received my name from a church member as a guest musician recommendation to lead a special music event they were having. This was the birth of a ministry that would span forty-plus years and take this little Baptist girl into numerous denominations, non-denominational churches, retreats, and special events. While God was taking me to all these places, He continued to use me as a church pianist or as a worship leader for contemporary worship services at my local church.

It did not take long for me to realize that God used the medium of music to get me in the door at different venues, but His purpose was more about the testimony I shared about the difference God had made in my life, particularly in overcoming life's hardships. God always worked a way for me to bring this encouragement into these opportunities, and it was evidenced in the tears on faces and words spoken to me after a service, speaking engagement, or music program. Although many people approached me in different ways for various reasons, there was a repeated theme shared privately with me that God spoke directly to them through me, and the message was timely for a struggle faced. Sometimes, however, God touched lives without my saying one word of testimony. I simply played the piano, but afterward I would hear this same "theme" repeated from a tear-stained face. It continues to amaze me how God can get His message delivered with or without words from me or any other human.

That is the blessing side of ministry, but there are two sides to every story, and mine is no exception. Along the way I encountered some of the most hurtful comments, judgments, harassments, and outright unsolicited confrontations by people who called themselves Christians. This happened a few times while standing in a church sanctuary, no less! The place it occurs does not make the impact better or worse, of course, because God is present everywhere to see and hear it all. He is the One whose opinion should matter to us. We humans, however, expect people to behave more reverently at least at church, right? In the grand scheme of things, the attackers were but a handful compared to armloads of encouragers, but that handful could be as toxic to me as biological warfare. The hateful-toned bullets, verbal assaults, false-accusation grenades, negative-letter bombs, and outright mocking taunts pelted my ministry in spiritual attack. It is easy to understand why people would leave the institution of "church" and never return, but let's read God's warnings and encouragement to believers about tribulation, even if it is precipitated by a person wearing the name of Christ:

> *Beloved, do not be surprised at the fiery ordeal among you, which comes upon you for your testing, as though some strange thing were happening to you; but to the degree that you share the sufferings of Christ, keep on rejoicing, so that also at the revelation of His glory you may rejoice with exultation. If you are reviled for the name of Christ, you are blessed, because the Spirit of glory and of God rests on you. (I Peter 4:12–14 NASB)*

> *These things I have spoken to you so that in Me you may have peace. In this world you have tribulation, but take courage; I have overcome the world. (John 16:33 NASB)*

Understanding that trials and tribulations are a part of life does not wipe away the fact that assaults hurt, remarks maim, gossip festers, snarky attitudes pour salt into wounds, and misrepresentations negatively impact a reputation. It is particularly disarming when it comes from a fellow Christian, who is supposed to know and act better. One day God showed me an empowering passage with a promise and a proper target:

> *Therefore, humble yourselves under the mighty hand of God, that He may exalt you at the proper time, casting all your anxiety on Him, because He cares for you. Be of sober spirit, be on the alert. Your adversary, the devil, prowls around like a roaring lion, seeking someone to devour. But resist him, firm in your faith, knowing that the same experiences of suffering are being accomplished by your brethren who are in the world. After you have suffered for a little while, the God of all grace, who called you to His eternal glory in Christ, will Himself perfect, confirm, strengthen and establish you. (I Peter 5:6–10 NASB)*

My adversary was Satan, not any of these haters. In fact, I needed to view these misguided Christians as deceived lambs in the lion's mouth being devoured as Satan used them for his puppets while harming them, though they were ignorant of their own wounds and numb to their pain. They might pummel my spirit, but that was no excuse to keep me from praying for them because they were in trouble without realizing it. In the next chapter, as we look at this passage in more depth and traverse the trenches and foxholes of spiritual warfare, I will share how I managed to keep my view of the real enemy and gain strength from God's promises.

If you come to God in this moment feeling not accepted, let me encourage you in the same way I encourage myself and regain my strength to persevere through difficult experiences. My hope and yours is found here, and I encourage you to spend time meditating on these powerful verses that remind us as children of God, we have been given Christ's overcoming power and His everlasting, abiding love.

> *And He has said to me, "My grace is sufficient for you, for power is perfected in weakness." Most gladly, therefore, I will rather boast about my weaknesses, so that the power of Christ may dwell in me. Therefore, I am well content with weaknesses, with insults, with distresses, with persecutions, with difficulties, for Christ's sake; for when I am weak, then I am strong. (2 Corinthians 12:9–10 NASB)*

| COME AS YOU'RE NOT |

But God demonstrates His own love toward us, that while we were yet sinners, Christ died for us. (Romans 5:8 NASB)

Remember God's cavalry I mentioned in the first paragraph of this chapter? Sometimes His cavalry is a dear friend or a stranger who speaks Truth into your spirit. Other times it is a whole platoon, like the time I was called to the church, where I served on staff, to meet with the pastor and a committee of people to address an issue that was deliberately misrepresented in order to hurt me. I was on a field trip with my son in a nearby city when I was asked via a phone call to report that night for the meeting. At that moment, I was not privy to the nature of the issue, but I could tell it must be something serious if my presence was required. I was about to walk into a meeting with no foreknowledge of my "sin." I told no one but my husband about the call, not even those with me on the field trip, and due to the trip's estimated return arrival time, I would be driving straight to the meeting with no chance to freshen up, change out of my field trip clothes, or gather my thoughts.

Somehow, the word leaked about the meeting and calls were made without my knowledge while I was away. People who loved me fought for me, but not against humans. Instead, they went straight to the Commander-in-Chief for help by organizing in the church choir loft at a specified time before my arrival. There they prayed to God for me and sang worship songs.

Driving to the church, I wondered if Daniel had felt a heavy heart like mine heading to the lion's den. As I exited my car at my destination and approached the church with a sinking feeling in the pit of my stomach, I thought I heard angels singing. I literally stopped in the parking lot to listen because I thought the stress was toying with my mind, but then

I realized I definitely heard the most beautiful voices. Nearing the building, I understood the lyrics of a familiar refrain, "God will take care of you, through every day, o'er all the way; He will take care of you; God will take care of you."

I don't know if you are familiar with that hymn, but the lyrics were perfect for my situation. For more than an hour before I arrived, these prayer warriors sang many songs, separated by prayers as people felt led. I know the timing of my arrival to hear that particular hymn guiding my steps was heaven-led. As I joined the cavalry in the sanctuary, learning what had transpired and how long they had been there praying and singing, they invited me to join them on all the verses before I attended that meeting. There, they wrapped their love and support around me like a soothing balm packing a powerful remedy as we sang with full, confident voices:

> Be not dismayed what e'er betide, God will take care of you;
> Beneath His wings of love abide, God will take care of you.
>
> Through days of toil when heart doth fail, God will take care of you;
> When dangers fierce your path assail, God will take care of you.
>
> All you may need He will provide, God will take care of you;
> Nothing you ask will be denied, God will take care of you.
>
> No matter what may be the test, God will take care of you;
> Lean, weary one, upon His breast, God will take care of you.

God did come through for me in a mighty way. He filled me with His peace and strength, level heads and open hearts were present, and everything worked out for the best for all concerned at that meeting. Like I Peter 5:10 promised, God exalted me at the proper time, as He confirmed, strengthened, and established me; not the kind of exalting that should be reserved for the Lord, but the kind that my Daddy in Heaven uses to make everything better for His child.

Today, I'm your cavalry with a book, Bible verses, and hymn lyrics in my arsenal, commissioned by our Commander-in-Chief. Come as you're not and nestle in your Heavenly Father's loving arms. Rest your head against His chest and listen to His heart beat the refrain of His never-ending acceptance of you.

Not Strong Enough

CHAPTER EIGHT

Therefore, humble yourselves under the mighty hand of God, that He may exalt you at the proper time, casting all your anxiety on Him, because He cares for you. Be of sober spirit, be on the alert. Your adversary, the devil, prowls around like a roaring lion, seeking someone to devour. But resist him, firm in your faith, knowing that the same experiences of suffering are being accomplished by your brethren who are in the world. After you have suffered for a little while, the God of all grace, who called you to His eternal glory in Christ, will Himself perfect, confirm, strengthen and establish you. (I Peter 5:6–10 NASB)

For our struggle is not against flesh and blood, but against the rulers, against the powers, against the world forces of this darkness, against the spiritual forces of wickedness in the heavenly places. (Ephesians 6:12 NASB)

Though spiritual warfare is real, there is no need to fear. We have a God who fights for us, and this is my story of God fighting one of my battles that I never knew was waged until it was too late. God was right on time, though. In fact, He had completed His recon mission, strategized on the intel, and implemented His plan without my knowledge.

Years ago, I attended a new Bible class in a nearby town. The Precept Bible Study employed an inductive study approach with five hours of homework per week and an hour class discussion covering our homework, which was followed immediately by another hour viewing a lecture video presented by Kay Arthur. After the initial class, I was hooked because for the first time, the Bible came alive and fascinated me. In one study session, the depth of my understanding improved tenfold and my appetite for learning was insatiable. On my way home that evening, I stopped by my friend Chris' house and said, "I just left the most amazing Bible study. I don't know what you have on Monday nights, but you need to rearrange your schedule and come with me. This is a life-changing opportunity." She took my advice and never regretted it. At the end of the semester we both were so passionate about the inductive study method that we enlisted in the next training session offered to become certified Precept teachers so we could start a study group in one of our area churches. Through word of mouth, the class grew and attracted women from various denominations. One day we lost our meeting place and had to relocate, which proved to be a bit challenging because we needed a site big enough for student table space that was equipped with a dry erase board and audio/visual capabilities large enough to be seen by an entire room.

    I contacted a local community college about renting a classroom weekly on Monday evenings because I knew different community groups often utilized this resource. The college was accommodating and all systems were a go. To advertise the class to any potential interested party among college staff and employees, I sent out a campus-wide email about the new Bible class starting on Monday nights, outlining the fee for the class, which covered the workbook and a share of the shipping cost, classroom rental, and video rental.

    Shortly thereafter, I was called to the office of one of the vice presidents. A couple of atheists on campus had filed a complaint that I was making money off a Bible class on a college campus, and they wanted the class removed in their concern for separation of church and state. I had to produce the resource catalog I used for ordering the materials and video so I could prove I was making no money off the class. The vice president then advised that while we could rent a room, I could only request a room for two weeks at a time, which meant I would need to call every two weeks to request a room and hope they were not all filled. In addition, while the college might have a room available every two weeks, there was no guarantee we would have the same room each time. In fact, it could and probably would change. Are you able to envision the problems this presented? With our large campus and its many parking areas, either I would need to call or assign a class member to call my students with the room number and building info every couple of weeks so they would know where to park and find us.

I decided the class and I could take on the extra challenges and trust God to save us a room. This was an opportunity to put into practice what we had learned from our last study about what it means to be in a covenant partnership with God. As our covenant partner, He fights for us and against our enemies. This is one reason why we can love our enemies and pray for them, rather than engage in a battle.

As I left the vice president's office a bit shaken that people on campus tried to have us removed and went so far as to complain to a vice president, something told me to check the availability of the president's board room for our class. I knew his office allowed outside groups use it from time to time. The president's secretary advised we were welcome to use it, but we would have to reserve it each week. We could not have a standing reservation. On top of that, one Monday night a month the college board of trustees met in that space, so we would be kicked out at least once a month. I decided to reserve it because having the same space at least three weeks of each month was better than moving all over the campus every two weeks. Again, we would put our trust in God to keep the space available to us and not let another group book it before we could.

Just when I thought everything was settled and I was about to cancel the other classroom reservation, those atheists on campus reared their heads again, this time with a different vice president. I was summoned to his office and he began a spiel that sounded very much like the issue reported to the other vice president. The atheists had failed to tell him that the matter had already been reported, discussed and settled with the other vice president. After some discussion back and forth, he finally said with an exasperated tone, "Well, you just can't have a Bible study in one of our classrooms. Period."

Actually, we aren't meeting in a classroom.

You're not? Where are you meeting?

In the president's board room.

Oh, well, he can do what he wants with that space.

YES! Yeah, God! I'm a little slow sometimes because not until this point did I realize a spiritual war was raging—and I was a tad late joining the battle. Our covenant partner heard every word of the atheists' plan and the deceit used with the second vice president. Meanwhile, that "something" that told me to check on the president's board room was more like a "Someone"—THEE Someone.

I had trouble waiting until the next Precept class to share all of this with them. God took our lesson on His covenant partnership and put a practical application to use. As you can imagine, the depth of our faith deepened another ten feet, but God was not finished yet. Remember that board meeting once a month on Monday nights? Out of the blue they changed their meeting time to noon on Mondays, which freed up the space the entire month. For over ten years, we reserved the board room every week and it was always available as we lived by faith that it would be there for us. We had the best accommodations on campus for free, complete with cushioned seats, huge board table, large dry-erase board, and theater-like audio/visual capabilities.

If this chapter finds you feeling the blows of a spiritual attack, I pray my story encourages you. If it has become more difficult to stand strong and persevere, I pray this message and the Scripture passages arrived just in time, but moreover, I join my voice with yours right now to our Commander-in-Chief, our Covenant Partner, the God Who Sees, the God Who Hears, our Avenger and Defender of the Brethren.

God has impressed me to pray for those who read this chapter because someone or several someones need this message. I will write it out below in this month of May, 2016. It is possible you are about to read a prayer that was written specifically on your behalf, or for someone you know, perhaps months or years before this book found its way to your hands; possibly penned before you knew there was a need for it until this time in your life. You have not escaped the notice of our Sovereign God, though. Join me in an attitude of prayer, and if possible, read aloud:

> *Almighty God, You have not given us a spirit of timidity but one of power, love and a sound mind. Our adversary is not content to wound us. He wants to annihilate families, shred dreams, crush hopes, devastate reputations, ruin finances, devour careers, inflict*

pain, gnaw on wounds, capture thoughts, and torture hearts through lies, deceit, guilt and doubt. By the power of Jesus' name, raise up this reader as Your valiant warrior. Renew strength, take back those captive thoughts as Your own, rewrite the script of this one's life, and give the reader a better story ending in accordance with Your will. Although this reader may come not strong, I trust that in this weakness Your strength is made perfect. May peace that only You can give resonate louder than any lie Satan would use to enslave any struggling one. In Jesus' name I pray, amen.

Not in a Good Place

CHAPTER NINE

There have been only a couple of workplaces in my employment life where someone made my days more difficult than they had to be. The worst place brought me eye-to-eye with pure evil inches away from my face.

Several years ago, I was excited to start my new job because not only would I be able to use my event planning and hospitality skills, but my boss seemed like a neat person in the interview process. For the sake of this chapter, I will give him the name Mr. Jones. We would be doing a lot of fundraising to help provide financial aid, and since community service was already a passion of mine, there appeared to be a nice fit.

During my first week, I was often approached by other employees from different departments to chat, but I noticed the same question would be thrown in there somewhere in the conversation, "So, how is it to work with Mr. Jones?" It made me wonder why everyone kept asking me that question, as I sensed an underlying issue, especially when a knowing smirk accompanied that question.

It did not take long for me to understand their curiosity because his facade soon came down and in its place arose temper flare-ups, overreactions, hateful talk about employees behind their backs after smiling to their faces, and the inability to cope well under pressure. Due to the nature of our department working on deadlines for events, that meant pressure most of the time and therefore his not-so-lovely attitude. Then I began to notice him doing unethical things that bordered on dishonesty.

I cannot talk about him without a fair assessment of myself. I engaged in gossiping about Mr. Jones with those employees who quizzed me about working with him in my first week. I came to learn they also had stories to tell about unpleasant encounters with Mr. Jones. Commiserating with them gave me a way to release steam and regroup, knowing someone else understood and agreed with me that he was an awful person. I tell you right now that my actions were as wrong in God's eyes as the actions of Mr. Jones, and at that time, I sort of suppressed that nagging tug of conviction because I felt I had every right to be upset. Hello? Can anyone out there identify and say an amen? Crickets? You are right. My behavior was shameful, and God was going to get me on my knees to pray for Mr. Jones one way or another soon.

At this point in my story, you may be wondering why God would deal with me for gossiping and promoting bad attitudes about my boss when Mr. Jones' behavior seemed much worse. Here's the deal. Mr. Jones was not a Christian, so why would God hold him to His high expectations? In fact, he was not a believer in any supreme being, but I was a child of God called to be salt and light in a dark world as I pressed on toward the high calling of God in Christ Jesus. There was no escape clause in God's command like, "Be salt and light unless you find yourself working with the spawn of Satan. In that event, you have a pass to gossip and help dig a deeper hole than he already dug for himself." Quite the contrary, here is what God commands of a believer:

| Come as You're Not |

> *You are the salt of the earth; but if the salt has become tasteless, how can it be made salty again? It is no longer good for anything, except to be thrown out and trampled underfoot by men. You are the light of the world. A city set on a hill cannot be hidden; nor does anyone light a lamp and put it under a basket, but on the lampstand, and it gives light to all who are in the house. Let your light shine before men in such a way that they may see your good works, and glorify your Father who is in heaven. (Matthew 5:13–16 NASB)*
>
> *I press on toward the goal unto the prize of the high calling of God in Christ Jesus. (Philippians 3:14 ASV)*

One day God used the worst of Mr. Jones to open my eyes to pray for him, rather than gossip about him, and it was a frightening encounter. We were working side by side, inches apart, sharing a computer monitor to search a database, casually chatting as we worked. Somehow the topic of televangelists came up. It went something like the following as Mr. Jones began:

> *All TV preachers are the same. They lie and steal money. They prey on old ladies and weak women to rob them of everything they have.*
>
> *I agree that some televangelists are crooks, but not all of them.*
>
> *Name one who isn't.*
>
> *Billy Graham. I think Billy Graham is honest to a fault, and he does not prey on people of any gender.*
>
> *Don't be fooled. He's just like the rest of them.*
>
> *I'm sorry. I have to respectfully disagree with you when it comes to Billy Graham.*

In a twinkling of an eye, Mr. Jones' whole countenance changed. He whipped his head to face me and leaned in with his jaw stiff and slightly jutted out, his upper lip snarled, the vein in his neck protruding, eyebrows furrowed, a look of disgust glaring from his eyes. His whole body language was extremely tensed. That was scary enough between the sudden and rapid head turn and the way he looked just inches from my face, but then he spoke. His voice was audibly different, and it did not sound like that of Mr. Jones. There was such a presence of evil in his tone and the lilted chatter was now deliberate and pronounced, "Weeell, I can tell you that Billy Graham is a..." I cannot repeat his lengthy tirade, but it was so vile I literally shuddered with goosebumps. Truly I had come face to face with pure evil in that moment.

As soon as he finished, his face changed back to his normal expression, he sat back in his chair, and with a change of subject, his usual speaking voice returned like nothing had happened. It was a noticeable transformation. I felt like I was in a movie where a demon possessed a body and then left the person.

I needed to pray for him. That was clear. I did not know how I could continue working in those conditions, but I also wanted to do what God would want. Perhaps I should stay and try to be a witness to Mr. Jones, but I battled my first instinct, which was to get out of Dodge on the next stagecoach. My fervent prayer went something like this:

> *Lord, please take hold of Mr. Jones' heart and change him, or change me to be able to work with him. Move him or move me. Change him or change me. I don't care how You do it, but I trust You realize something has to give.*

Within a month, Mr. Jones took another job and did not even tell me about his decision to leave until the day he walked out the door. I had already heard it from others, however, and planned an open house at my office for the next week to usher in a more welcoming reception with the changing of the guard. Praise be to God for taking care of my problem, but not only for me. I have no doubt Mr. Jones moved to a place that was a better fit for him as well.

Who comes to mind when you read this chapter? Is the message for you, a friend, a family member? Maybe the place that is not good is your home. Perhaps you are in a relationship that is not in a good place. Spend a moment seeking God's counsel about how to pray for the situation and how you can bring salt and light to it. Ask God to search your heart and reveal if this place is His best for you. Be prepared to hear your own shortcomings, if any, and engage your free will to make changes as He directs. Dare to come not in a good place and give God the opportunity to remedy the problem.

Not Feeling God's Love

CHAPTER TEN

I write a blog called, "After the Lemonade." We've all heard it said that when life gives you lemons, make lemonade. I do not know about you, but I have made the lemonade many times and still had lemons left over. What do you do then, especially when the lemons are the moldy, vile, disgusting variety arriving by the truckload? Thus, was born the idea for my platform for hope and encouragement, "After the Lemonade."

A friend of mine had been pelted with many a lemon in her life, and one day I sensed the Lord sending me on a God-ordained rescue attempt for the purpose of providing encouragement and Scripture. It all started when I noticed she had not been her usual chatty self for several days, which was unlike her. Something in my spirit told me to check on her. I felt an alarm bell go off in my heart, and as God would have it, my friend's cell phone number was already in my address book, no doubt planted on me for such a time as this. With that phone call, I embarked as God's agent on a rescue mission, whose ending is still being written by God as I pen our story in this chapter.

My friend was in a deep pit, feeling like God not only abandoned her but actually turned on her in anger and disgust, causing terrible things to happen as punishment. It was not my friend's first time to feel conflicted about God's love. She was angry with God and could not hear Him respond to her pleas, which she interpreted as confirmation of her suspicions.

Down in the pit, it is impossible to get a clear perspective. My sweet friend needed someone outside the pit to reach down and help her climb out, especially since the wastewater of negative thoughts ran so deep, they caused her to tread in the cesspool of stinking thinking to stay afloat. She could not keep that up forever and was going down fast. From everything that had happened in her decades of living, I understood why she could have her perspective skewed about God. How did I know that? Because I was familiar with Satan's warfare tactics. He was not referenced without reason as the father of lies (John 8:44), a deceiver (Revelation 12:9) and an accuser of the brethren (Revelation 12:10).

This was a complex situation because my friend viewed God as unforgiving of her past mistakes, yet she could counsel another with the assurance that God will forgive if you ask Him. She felt punished by God due to terrible incidents allowed in her life, causing her to question if God still or ever loved her. Meanwhile, she reached out to complete strangers as well as friends to minister to them with all the words a Christian would use to convey God's love and provision. In short, my friend could not apply her own advice to herself. Despite her earnest prayers to hear God, the silence from heaven fell on her ears as loveless rejection. Worse, when a trial hit, she slipped into a well-worn rut of a self-deprecating dialogue listing all the reasons God had forsaken her, how miserable her entire existence was, and how she was a worthless individual of no value to anyone, undeserving of any consideration. What a pack of lies this lamb of God believed, as she was being led to the slaughterhouse of dreams and joy.

Come as You're Not

Satan had convinced my friend that God could stop loving her, and Satan deceived her further with this lie to steal her joy, devastate her hope, and skew her perspective about God by twisting truth with deception and accusations. Then, at the moment she was ready to give up and turn her back on the Lord, God threw her a lifeline by prompting me to reach out to her. Over several weeks, long talks and longer texts, God attempted to put my friend's life back together and heal her wounds. Sure, there were setbacks, but God never gave up on her and neither did I. She had not gotten this way overnight, and the healing process would not happen overnight. Little by little, God worked at opening her blind eyes with the message that He already proved His love for her way back before the creation of the world when the plan to save mankind through Jesus was devised. The plan would have failed if Jesus had not lived without sinning His entire life to become our spotless Lamb. It would have failed if Jesus had not gone through with His mission all the way to the cross, grave, and resurrection. Laying down His life for us proved the matchless love of God the Father and God the Son.

Nothing my friend could do or say would make God love her more because His love bank was already filled to overflowing. He had seen her at her worst before the creation of the world, He loved her completely and perfectly in spite of it, His love remained unfazed, and God still sent Jesus to lay down His life for my misguided friend. None of her sins and shortcomings surprised God as they unfolded, so they could never cause God to love her less.

I reminded my friend that she needed to understand the difference between guilt and conviction. Satan uses guilt to keep us down by bringing to mind everything we do wrong, outlining why God could not possibly love or forgive us in light of that. He accuses and tattles on us before God, all in an attempt to push our heads under the waters of sin and despair to drown hope. Satan had convinced my precious friend of a pack of lies to destroy her.

On the other hand, God convicts us about our sin so we can address it, ask forgiveness, receive mercy, find freedom from the slavery to sin, and soar to new joy-filled heights, using hope for fuel. God demonstrated His love and forgiveness so we may come to Him without fear to find mercy and grace in time of need. He rescues us through conviction for the purpose of keeping our heads above water to sail on the sea of His full life, and this is what He wanted for my friend. It is what He wants for you and me, too.

My friend needed to rescue her thoughts from the rut, renew her mind, rewrite her dialogue script, and remind herself of God's merciful promise offered to anyone who would accept His free gift of grace through Jesus Christ:

> *If we confess our sins, He is faithful and righteous to forgive us our sins and to cleanse us from all unrighteousness. (I John 1:9 NASB)*

She needed to remember that God showed the entire world how much He loved us.

> *For God so loved the world that he gave his only begotten Son, that whosoever believeth in him should not perish, but have everlasting life. (John 3:16 KJV)*

> *Just as the Father has loved Me, I have also loved you; abide in My love. (John 15:9 NASB)*

> *See how great a love the Father has bestowed on us, that we would be called children of God; and such we are. For this reason the world does not know us, because it did not know Him. (I John 3:1 NASB)*

This is love: not that we loved God, but that he loved us and sent his Son as an atoning sacrifice for sins. (I John 4:10 NIV)

Plus, my friend needed a reminder that just because one cannot see any evidence of God at work, that does not mean He is idle. I am obsessed with the following verse which reminds me how God can be at work doing huge, miraculous things unseen by us.

The waters saw you, God, the waters saw you and writhed; the very depths were convulsed. The clouds poured down water, the heavens resounded with thunder; your arrows flashed back and forth. Your thunder was heard in the whirlwind, your lightning lit up the world; the earth trembled and quaked. Your path led through the sea, your way through the mighty waters, **though your footprints were not seen.** *(Psalm 77:16–19 NIV, emphasis mine)*

Have you ever been in my friend's situation or known someone in the pit of writhing, convulsing, thunderous turmoil? Is your shaken world quaking from the cannons of repeated assault? God has not finished writing the story of our lives, and we have to give Him time to work. He beckons us to come as we're not, unable to trace His hand at work, unable to hear from heaven, unable to feel His love. Come even if nothing you see looks like love to you. Come if you tried in the past to be close to God but never felt Him come through for you. Simply come trusting God's heart *for* you. Be still and for as long as it takes, refocus your thoughts on believing that God's heart is indeed for you, not against you.

> **Remind yourself of God's promises, and rest in the renewal that comes from a speck of faith in the shadow of a cross of love.**
> **—Micah Duckett**

Not Able to Let It Go

CHAPTER ELEVEN

Why is forgiveness such a challenge to gift and re-gift? Most of us appreciate the receiving end of the exchange, but the donating part can prove too costly. In the case of an egregious wrong, forgiveness is attached at the hip to 'impossible'. Self-help books on the topic of forgiveness continue to fill the shelves of bookstores and libraries but often do not defray the price demanded for offering a gift so selfless. In today's world of technology, electronic books on the subject arrive in our hands within a minute or two without leaving our chairs, but the time and expense saved are of no value at times in the grand scheme of things. Search engines make it possible in private Bible study to research the Hebrew or Greek translations for the word *forgiveness*—Hebrew for the Old Testament and Greek for the New Testament—something that once required the lugging of separate tomes to one's study area. With all these modern conveniences at our disposal and thousands of words of advice on the topic, the struggle to forgive a wrong persists, relentless in its pursuit of mankind's emotions and thoughts.

Like a rite of passage, at some point each of us must face the forgiveness gift exchange, and sometimes the swap is one-sided, often beginning in our early years. I remember when one of my sons participated in a grade school gift exchange. We wrapped up a cool toy for our gift to give, and it happened to be one he really wanted for himself. Finally, the day of the party arrived, and my son was anxious to see what cool toy someone would give him. Wouldn't it be awesome if he received the same toy we gave to someone else? Ripping into the paper like a contestant in a timed race, my son's countenance changed drastically as the curled edges of dingy, used, math flash cards emerged. It was bad enough to receive flash cards, but used flash cards were the worst. My heart sank with his momentarily, but I quickly regrouped at the thought of some child's embarrassment to find it necessary to give a classmate this gift. It was probably all they could afford, so I hastened to whisper in my son's ear to be gracious and thank the other child, as I promised to take him shopping for that toy he wanted after school. I was proud of him for putting on a brave face, and later we talked more about the other child's circumstances. While he understood, it still did not take away the disappointment of the moment. As adults, we can relate to that life lesson.

There is nothing humorous nor is there any comparison, however, between a grade school gift swap and the harm inflicted in more serious exchanges. In my years of mentoring, I have wept at the stories of physical abuse inflicted by someone who should have been trustworthy, a bank account emptied when a spouse suddenly walked out on the family, a botched surgery that left the patient disabled, the brutal murder of fine Christian grandparents by their own grandchild in a home invasion robbery, and the attempted sexual assault of an adolescent by a teacher, to name a few.

If you have read the Bible, you may have seen some examples of God's take on forgiveness and love from Scripture, such as the following:

> *Be kind and compassionate to one another, forgiving each other, just as in Christ, God forgave you. (Ephesians 4:32 NIV)*
> ★ *Note the measure of forgiveness defined in that verse: "...just as in Christ, God forgave you."*

> *Be completely humble and gentle; be patient, bearing with one another in love. (Ephesians 4:2 NIV)*

> *It does not dishonor others, it is not self-seeking, it is not easily angered, it keeps no record of wrongs. (I Corinthians 13:5 NIV, speaking about love)*

> *But I tell you, love your enemies and pray for those who persecute you, that you may be children of your Father in heaven. He causes his sun to rise on the evil and the good, and sends rain on the righteous and the unrighteous. (Matthew 5:44–45 NIV)*

> *Do not judge. For in the same way you judge others, you will be judged, and with the measure you use, it will be measured to you. (Matthew 7:1–2)*

Believers and non-believers alike understand that forgiveness does not excuse bad behavior, and it does not mean we no longer consider the offense to be wrong. We understand that forgiveness does not equate to forgetting the wrong ever happened. "Forgive and forget" is attributed to God, but it is not actually in the Bible at all. Nowhere does God tell us we must forget while we forgive. Would forgetting help us move forward more swiftly and reach a better place emotionally? Probably so, but it is absolutely possible to never forget while not allowing it to eat at us or cause a root of bitterness to anchor in our hearts. How can we do that?

As I prayed about this chapter and sought God's wisdom, He reminded me that centuries ago He addressed the subject of forgiveness and had to make this choice before He ever spoke a word into Creation. After He saw the worst moments of our future, God had to exercise forgiveness for each human being for all time before He ever uttered, "Let there be light." Stop and contemplate what that might have looked like when He considered you. God took time to examine every moment of your life before the first human being was created. He heard your every thought, listened to every word, and saw every action, reaction and sin of your entire life. Then He said, "No, I don't see anything here that I cannot forgive or would make Me change My mind about creating the universe and offering salvation to this person, although I have to admit I was pretty tempted. Are You willing to suffer and die for this person, Jesus? Okay, good. We are in agreement. Now let's examine the next human."

We touched on the subject in a prior chapter, but allow me to quote the passage here again as we look to God's own example to guide us:

> Blessed be the God and Father of our Lord Jesus Christ, who has blessed us with every spiritual blessing in the heavenly places in Christ, just as **He chose** us in Him **before the foundation of the world**, that we would be holy and blameless before Him. (Ephesians 1:3–4 NASB, emphasis mine)

God made a choice to offer forgiveness to His offenders—that is you and me. We have a choice as well to follow His example. Here is the secret to the formula. When we make the choice to let go of bitterness and wounded feelings, we also let go of their control, which releases the burden they cause. The Koine Greek *aphesis* used for forgiveness is defined as "a sending away, a letting go, a release."[1] Forgiving enables us to let go

---

[1] Strong's Exhaustive Concordance 859

of the pain of the reminder (a letting go), and as we send the pain away (a sending away), we find ourselves delivered from the hold it had over our lives (a release). I don't know about you, but I think God was and remains brilliant in His choice of words when I see that definition for forgiveness, which dates back centuries ago. To ensure our success at forgiving and empower us to follow through with it, Jesus imparts His own overcoming power to us through faith.

> *For everyone born of God overcomes the world. This is the victory that has overcome the world, even our faith. (I John 5:4 NIV)*
>
> *But thanks be to God! He gives us the victory through our Lord Jesus Christ. (I Corinthians 15:57 NIV)*
>
> *I have told you these things, so that in me you may have peace. In this world you will have trouble. But take heart! I have overcome the world. (John 16:33 NIV)*
>
> *No, in all these things we are more than conquerors through Him who loved us. (Romans 8:37 NIV)*

If we hang on to unforgiveness, we make a choice to nurture a deadly cancer that will ultimately devour the heart. Here's a word picture for you. Imagine the doctor tells you a deadly form of cancer is growing on your heart, but it can be removed with no harm to you. In fact, once removed, you will feel not only much improved, but you will function better in your daily life instead of struggling to get through the day or enduring frequent heart attacks. Then you reply:

> **Simply put, forgiveness prevents bad behavior from destroying our hearts.**
> **Micah Duckett**

> Oh no, I could never bring myself to have that surgery. I am fine with keeping that cancer right where it is. I understand it causes me pain which could be remedied in short order. While I would have a better quality of life if the cancer was removed, I do not mind sacrificing those things in order to function as I've grown accustomed. After all, suffering has become a place of comfort for me. Like I have done time and again, I can deal with episodes of pain when they arise, even though I am aware that doing so negatively impacts other areas of my life. I have managed all these years by not thinking about it or dealing with it; what's a few more? If the cancer eats away at my heart, well, so be it because that is better than going through surgery.

As ridiculous as that word picture reads, *I wonder if our refusing to forgive reads to God, our great physician, in the same ridiculous way?*

Consider this. If you are honest with yourself, is there any acceptable excuse that comes to mind for not forgiving, which you could present to God when you stand before Him one day to give an account for your disobedience to forgive? Seriously, take a moment to imagine.

> It is your turn to come forward and stand before God. Look into the face of the One who witnessed all your sins, from the vilest to the most petty. Now look at the right hand of God where Jesus sits, and study His scarred body tortured for your petty sins as well as your most vile offenses. Is that your name engraved in that one scar across His heart? Pause to remember how Jesus poured out His life as a drink offering to ransom you. Nothing asked of Him was too great---not the torture, not the humiliation, and not the rejection and abandonment. See the blood of Jesus smeared on the mercy seat of God to atone for your "shortcomings?" I think I see your name written in blood there on that seat. Look around you. Witness the throng of believers tortured and maimed for their faith who found the fortitude to forgive their offenders.

| Come as You're Not |

Can you honestly imagine any scenario where God would say:

> *Wow! How did I miss that? You were treated wrong, beyond any expectation of forgiveness, and way worse than Jesus. Let Me fall on My knees and apologize to you for expecting you to be able to move past that! Jesus is God, but You are only human. Well, sure, Jesus did take on human flesh to experience every temptation that any human encounters, but even HE barely moved past something similar when it happened to Him. Leave all your baggage here except that one bag of unforgiveness. You have My permission to take it with you into heaven in the event you run into your offender up here. Please forgive* **ME** *for expecting too much of you.*

Whatever you may have endured at the hands of another, does it now seem pretty juvenile and short-sighted to think there could be any comparison between the offenses to you and the offenses to God the Father, God the Son, God the Holy Spirit, and our martyred brothers and sisters in Christ? If you take up your cross and follow Christ, then that means sacrificing, loving your enemies, cutting people some grace who did not earn it, being generous with mercy, and offering forgiveness even when it is not merited. And that is just for starters.

Maybe you have been fortunate to escape the receiving end of an egregious offense, but you struggle today to maintain a relationship with someone you need to forgive for something less life-impacting. Perhaps the offender is not aware of the wound inflicted to ask your forgiveness. Was something worded in a hurtful way or spoken with a bad tone? Maybe you feel somewhat slighted by not being included in an invitation, or someone took a side opposed to yours in an argument. I have experienced this with both friends and family dynamics, as most of us have if we're honest. In those moments of trivial offenses, I have to ask myself several questions, such as:

Do I want to have a relationship with this person or be right?

Is nurturing my wounds worth never speaking to this person again?

Which is greater: my love *for* this person or my wounds *from* this person?

What does the Bible call the greatest of these? Love. (I Corinthians 13:13 NIV)

What does the Bible say covers over all wrongs? Love (Proverbs 10:12 NIV)

Someone has to be the hero, sacrifice the claim to the "I'm right prize," and move forward. Someone's love—if not for the other person, then for God—has to outweigh what Satan meant for harm. We know one of Satan's tactics is to attack relationships in order to destroy them, so we cannot let him have the victory because when it comes right down to it, our offenders and we are ultimately on the same side—opposing Satan. If I have to choose between my family and friends versus Satan's winning by destroying relationships, I am always going to assume the position of protecting my loved ones.

Will you be the hero of your story? Will you fight for your family and friends, or will you concede the victory to Satan as you lie down and nurse your wounds? It won't be easy, but most things worthwhile are not.

> *Come to God as you're not, and leave the hero you were meant to be.*
> *Micah Duckett*

Almighty God, as I pen these words from Your heart, I know You already see the souls in turmoil and hear the pleas for deliverance. While unforgiveness may be tied at the hip of impossible, we know that nothing is impossible with You. Raise up an army of heroes to restore relationships. Resurrect love grown cold and reignite the original match of unity. Rekindle the fire of friendship and rebuild trust in time. In the cases of life-impacting wrongs, move in the hearts of the offenders and those inflicted to revive truth, honor, respect, and remorse as applicable. Empower the life-impacting afflicted to rise from the pit of filth; shame; condemnation; judgment; betrayal; and vile, disgusting actions. As you extend Your lifeline, O Lord, join them in the ascent from the pit, and allow them to feel the strength of Your presence taking them one handhold over the other at a time. Spread Your safety net of life-affirming love under these pit climbers so that if one should slip and fall, the security of Your safety net will break the impact and protect from further harm. Take back what Satan meant for calculated devastation, and replenish love banks with large deposits of Your overcoming power and life-affirming love for each reader praying this prayer along with me in earnest. You know even now, O Lord, who they are and why they find themselves in this place. We acknowledge that any victory is Yours because You set the example centuries ago for forgiveness, as You equipped us with the capacity to forgive as You did in Christ Jesus, in whose name I pray. Amen.

Not Recognizing God's Voice

CHAPTER TWELVE

As my faith grew, it became more and more important to check in with God to make sure I was on the right path for my future. Staying centered in His plans for my day-to-day living took on a higher priority level, but decision-making especially brought me to God's throne, asking for direction in accordance with His will. Here is an amazing story of how God answered one of those prayers.

For weeks I had been praying about an important decision, and I was somewhat paralyzed from moving forward with confidence because I was afraid of making a mistake. If you read Chapter Six, "Not Getting It Right," you understand my track record had not always been on point. I hear that unsolicited "Amen to that," but I forgive you.

The time to give an answer neared, and I confidentially prayed something like this:

> Lord, You've heard me say what I think I should do. If I have Your blessing to move forward because I am right on track with Your plan for my life, please make it clear to me in some supernatural, unexplainable-apart-from-You type of way. Show me You bless this decision by using a way that is a blessing as only You and I would understand it to be, so I can be sure it is not a coincidence.

| Micah Ann Duckett |

At the same time as all this was happening, Mike and I were scheduled to be a part of a team of lay leaders from different churches and cities for a renewal weekend at a church out of town. People from other churches in that city would attend the renewal weekend as well. They were strangers to us in the beginning, but friends in the end, though maybe not by name for each and every person. I was scheduled to play the piano for the event and lead a break-out group, and Mike was slated to lead a break-out group. The team would be staying in the homes of church members unknown to us, which always proved to be a rewarding experience where we left feeling more like family than houseguests.

At these events, the host church would coordinate with a local bookstore to create an on-site bookstore in the church lobby, fellowship hall, or nearby on campus so that attendees could peruse and purchase recommended reading material, magnets with inspirational messages, cute tee shirts, bookmarks, and so forth. This event would be no different, and I always looked forward to checking out the bookstore to see if I might find something I could not live without. Men reading this chapter may not get that concept of not being able to live without something that catches the eye, but most of the female audience is nodding with understanding smiles.

Prepare yourself for what you are about to read. It is so amazing you might fall off your seat, so consider yourself warned. Off we went to the renewal weekend, and I was still privately waiting for God to confirm that my decision was correct. Remember, I was in a place where I knew no one but the team members, and even the team had no clue about the decision confirmation I sought. During a break, I went to the makeshift bookstore in the lobby, and as I flipped through a book, I sensed someone had moved to stand beside me. Then

I heard a female voice say, "God told me to give you this." I turned to look to my right to see if she was talking to me, and I realized her arms were extended toward me, so I glanced down to see what she was now placing in my hand I was extending without realizing it. There lay a Precious Moments Bible.

For those who have never heard of the Precious Moments line of collectibles, the creator uses child-like figures to convey inspirational messages and capture the precious moments in our lives. I happened to collect Precious Moments figurines—owning a collection of over 300 at that time—and had longingly eyed that Precious Moments Bible for months but could not justify the purchase because I already owned several Bibles. Plus, this one was more for children than adults, but I loved the pictures in it. That did not seem like a good reason to spend money possibly needed elsewhere, so I just admired it from afar.

The second I realized a desire of my heart had been placed in my hand by a stranger who did not know I collected Precious Moments and could not know I wanted the Precious Moments Bible but presented me with something only God and I could know was a blessing to me, my heart leapt with joy. "I knew that I knew that I knew" God had just handed me my decision confirmation through this stranger, obedient to act as she felt led by God. It takes many words and lines of script to write this, but understand, all this happened in the space of less than five seconds. That is being generous because it was probably more like three seconds, tops. Second 1, I looked down. Second 2, I made the connection. Second 3, I immediately looked up to tell her with excitement that she had no idea how God had just used her to answer a prayer of mine to confirm a decision I had to make...

but she was gone!

You read that right. In less than five seconds—and more like three—she was nowhere to be found. I searched the lobby quickly. I asked people around me if they had seen "that lady who just left the table," to no avail. Our encounter was so brief, I could not recall her features, hair color, clothing—nothing except her voice sounded female. She had simply disappeared. I have a feeling she was an angel, but even if she was a human being, God used whoever or whatever to hand me a blessing, which only God knew I wanted, as the confirmation to move forward with my decision in answer to my prayer. The moment could only be explained as God-orchestrated.

That is one example of many times in my life I like to call "I knew that I knew that I knew" God was communicating with me. Here's another one. I was driving home, and in the distance, I noticed a young man and woman knocking on a church door and then looking in the windows. Apparently, the church was locked and no one answered their knocks. As I passed, they stepped into an adjoining open field about the size of a city block, presumably to cross through it. They appeared to be in their late teens, possibly early twenties. Their wrinkled clothing, disheveled hair, backpacks and a plastic grocery bag with clothing hanging out of it made me think they might be living on the street. I sensed God telling me to buy them a hamburger.

> *But God, by the time I reach a drive-thru, wait for my order to be filled, and then return to where I last saw them, they could be long gone. Not to mention I would have spent money on food I don't need.*

> *Go get the hamburgers.*

> *But God, how do I even know what they like on their hamburgers? Should I cut the onions? Do they prefer mayo or mustard? I don't*

know what kind of soda to get them. This is a waste of time and money.

Go get the food. They will be glad to eat whatever you get. Trust me.

At this point in the story, you may think I'm a nut case. Maybe so, and I am too far gone to recognize it, but maybe I'm not weird at all. God says His sheep know His voice. Read what God teaches us through Jesus' words in the book of John:

> "Truly, truly, I say to you, he who does not enter by the door into the fold of the sheep, but climbs up some other way, he is a thief and a robber. But he who enters by the door is a shepherd of the sheep. To him the doorkeeper opens, and the sheep hear his voice, and he calls his own sheep by name and leads them out. When he puts forth all his own, he goes ahead of them, and the **sheep follow him because they know his voice**. A stranger they simply will not follow, but will flee from him, because they do not know the voice of strangers." This figure of speech Jesus spoke to them, but they did not understand what those things were which He had been saying to them. So Jesus said to them again, "Truly, truly, I say to you, I am the door of the sheep. All who came before Me are thieves and robbers, but the sheep did not hear them. I am the door; if anyone enters through Me, he will be saved, and will go in and out and find pasture. The thief comes only to steal and kill and destroy; I came that they may have life, and have it abundantly. I am the good shepherd; the good shepherd lays down His life for the sheep. He who is a hired hand, and not a shepherd, who is not the owner of the sheep, sees the wolf coming, and leaves the sheep and flees, and the wolf snatches them and scatters them. He flees because he is a hired hand and is not concerned about the sheep. I am the good shepherd, and **I know My own and My own know Me**, even as the Father knows Me and I know the Father; and I lay down My life for the sheep. **I have other sheep, which are not of this fold; I must bring them also, and they will hear My voice; and**

they will become one flock with one shepherd." (John 10:1–16 NASB, emphasis mine)

If you are a child of God who has committed your life to Christ as Savior, then Jesus is your Shepherd, who acts as God instructs and speaks what God tells Him to say.

> For this reason therefore the Jews were seeking all the more to kill Him, because He not only was breaking the Sabbath, but also was calling God His own Father, making Himself equal with God. Therefore Jesus answered and was saying to them, "Truly, truly, I say to you, **the Son can do nothing of Himself, unless it is something He sees the Father doing; for whatever the Father does, these things the Son also does in like manner.** For the Father loves the Son, and shows Him all things that He Himself is doing; and the Father will show Him greater works than these, so that you will marvel. For just as the Father raises the dead and gives them life, even so the Son also gives life to whom He wishes. For not even the Father judges anyone, but He has given all judgment to the Son, so that all will honor the Son even as they honor the Father. He who does not honor the Son does not honor the Father who sent Him. Truly, truly, I say to you, he who hears My word, and believes Him who sent Me, has eternal life, and does not come into judgment, but has passed out of death into life." (John 5:18–24 NASB, emphasis mine)

> And Jesus cried out and said, "He who believes in Me, does not believe in Me but in Him who sent Me. He who sees Me sees the One who sent Me. I have come as Light into the world, so that everyone who believes in Me will not remain in darkness. If anyone hears My sayings and does not keep them, I do not judge him; for I did not come to judge the world, but to save the world. He who rejects Me and does not receive My sayings, has one who judges him; the word I spoke is what will judge him at the last day. **For I did not speak on My own initiative, but the Father Himself who sent Me has given Me a commandment as to what to say**

*and what to speak. I know that His commandment is eternal life; therefore **the things I speak, I speak just as the Father has told Me**." (John 12:44–50 NASB, emphasis mine)*

If you believe that Jesus was sent to earth by God to atone for your sins by becoming your sacrificial lamb, and you have committed your life to Him in faith after repenting of your sins, then Jesus is your Shepherd and you are one of His sheep. You have the capability to hear God speak through Jesus' voice. It is not an audible voice, though it can be, and it is hard to explain to someone who has not practiced listening for it or who is not a child of God and is therefore at a disadvantage. It should be stated, however, that God will not ask you to do something that He forbids or frowns upon. For instance, God will not tell you to harm yourself or commit a sin. Also, God can do anything, so if He wants You to hear His voice, He can make that happen, child of His or not.

I will attempt to describe how I recognize God's voice, but understand, it may be a little different for others. Compare it to a lightbulb or "aha" moment when you suddenly understand or figure out something. When that moment of understanding happens to me, not only is it clear what I am to do or what He is saying, but also my heart beats a little faster, which some people refer to as the quickening of the Spirit.

Perhaps it would be easier to grasp if you understood the relationship of a shepherd and the sheep. Back in Biblical times, a city had a large sheepfold available for shepherds who had to bring their sheep to town. The one sheepfold could hold several herds of sheep, and although they intermingled, there was no worry that the wrong sheep would accidentally follow the wrong shepherd out of the pen. The sheep only answered the call of their shepherd and would not leave with anyone but their shepherd. Why? They knew their shepherd's voice.

I knew my Shepherd's voice that day, and reluctantly I drove off to buy hamburgers, fries and soft drinks. It turned out to be a good thing that I trusted my Shepherd's voice because not only did I find them rather easily even though they had left the field, I discovered they had not eaten in a couple of days and were hoping to get food in trade for doing an odd job or two around that church they had been scoping out. With tears flowing down their cheeks, they shared their story of going on the road for Jesus with just a few personal belongings and their Bibles, which they proudly pulled from that plastic bag of clothing and pumped in the air a couple of times. It was their practice to accept no monetary handouts without working for it. We had a pleasant conversation, and then things got serious again after a brief pause when they said they had almost given up hope of God helping them find food, thinking it was partial punishment for mistakes of the past, when I came along with a meal saying, "God told me to get this for you."

God wanted me to write this chapter in my book because He wants to be noticed and heard while growing your faith through His lead-and-follow design. I would not be surprised if Your Shepherd is giving you that "I know that I know that I know" this is for me moment. Some of you are believers who haven't practiced recognizing when God is trying to talk to you. Still others may doubt that any of this is possible. Whatever your viewpoint, come take time to sit at Jesus' feet in prayer. Be still and know that He is also God the Son, and He is ready to be heard. All you need is a mustard seed of faith to "know that you know that you know" God is communicating with you.

I would love to know your story if God has used this chapter to open your heart to hear Him better or if you have a testimony to share in this regard. Write me at my website to briefly share your experience if you are so led.

Not Alone

Epilogue

Our time together closes with a celebration of our Savior's presence and purpose in our lives. With meticulous attention to detail and focused precision, the Lord used the good and bad circumstances throughout my lifetime to further His Kingdom agenda and allow me the privilege to witness His orchestration and share it with you in these pages.

I will never forget the day I met the pastor at a local Episcopal church. At the recommendation of a church member, he invited me to a meeting at his office to discuss the first of several weekly special music services leading up to Lent. Each special service would be planned and led by a guest musician, and I was asked to kick it off.

Right off the bat, following a brief introduction and pleasantries, he announced, "Now, I don't want any rah-rah music." A few moments of awkward silence followed, as I searched his facial expression for some clue about what that meant. I was not sure if he wanted feedback from me, but ultimately I asked, "By rah-rah, do you mean contemporary music?" I smile now, reminiscing about hitting the nail on the head and reassuring him that I would be respectful of their traditions if I incorporated a contemporary song in the service, but most of it would be hymns.

Grabbing one of their hymnals, I headed for home to see if

I might locate some hymns I knew for the purpose of finding common ground. My worship service planning custom is to begin with prayer because God knows what He wants to hear from us, and He is aware of the needs of those who will attend the service. God impresses on me what Scriptures to use and testimony to give as I incorporate the music in my plans. Soon tailor-made service plans emerge, and I pray over those plans.

Finally, the big day arrived, and I trusted God with all that He had impressed on me, including the two contemporary praise songs I planned to introduce. I noticed as we moved through the service that the pastor was raising his hands in worship and crying. The fleeting thought came to me: *For someone who did not want anything too rah-rah, that sure resembles what you see in a contemporary service.*

The next day, the pastor called and booked me for every one of those pre-Lent services. It pleased me that we had moved from that initial skeptical meeting to a place of trust and mutual respect. Each week God moved mightily, and there was plenty of good feedback and life-impacting responses.

At the close of the final service, the pastor called Mike and me forward. It was a complete surprise. I sat in a chair that he had pulled to the center of the platform, unaware of what was to follow. Then he invited all the congregation to come forward to lay hands on me, and they were instructed that if I could not be reached, they were to lay their hands on the person in front of them, creating a patchwork blanket covering made of hands, love and prayers. The pastor anointed my head with oil and prayed for God to bless my ministry. There I sat, a little Baptist girl in an Episcopal church getting her head anointed with oil and prayed over by an Episcopal pastor, who had allowed this stranger to come into his church to plan and lead a worship service. Our relationship began with concern about rah-rah music and ended with oil on my head. I could not orchestrate this blessing. Only God moves in the hearts of people like this.

I cannot forget to tell you about the time I was asked to lead worship for the local ministerial alliance, comprised of pastoral leadership from churches of many denominations and a couple of non-denominational churches. This was particularly daunting for me at first blush because there were so many different worship styles, religions, cultures, and ethnic backgrounds. I did not know how some of the clergy would feel about a woman leading them in worship, and besides that, who was insignificant I to lead such a group of seasoned, distinguished saints anywhere, much less in worship? So how did I handle this dilemma? I hit my spiritual knees in prayer because I knew only God could help me find the common ground to make our voices unite in worship.

Though I was terribly nervous at first, I soon settled down as we moved through the service that night. I looked across that room and saw worship expressed in many ways, some with bowed heads, others with outstretched arms, faces with smiles, faces with tears, faces with eyes closed, faces looking to heaven. Truly we stood on holy ground because the presence of the Lord filled that place, and we were one in heart, soul, mind, and strength.

The most moving moment came when we sang "Amazing Grace." They had been instructed to read through the first four of five verses of the song to pick the one verse that best described their testimony. Everyone would sing on all the verses, whether seated or standing, but they were to remain seated until we sang their testimony verse. At that time, they were to rise to their feet still singing, remain standing during that verse, and then sit down as we moved to the next verse. On we would go until we reached the fifth verse, "When we've been there ten thousand years, bright shining as the sun, we've no less days to sing God's praise, than when we'd first begun." On that verse, everyone would stand and sing with their whole heart as loud as they could, much like we would stand united in worship in heaven one day—people from different backgrounds united in a common love of God the Father, God the Son, and God the Holy Spirit.

Those ministers wept, and it was quite powerful to witness little groups stand on the various verses, some with arms around neighbors' shoulders. Up and down the bodies moved at their appropriate testimony verse until finally we came to that fifth verse, and I could hear all those chairs moving and feet standing like an army coming to attention. I wish I had the words to tell you how powerful it was, for I could feel their firm conviction through their voices. It was palpable, and soon my tears joined theirs. I knew we were not done, so I added a verse singing only the words *Praise God* over and over to the "Amazing Grace" tune. I modulated up in key again and again, with a dynamic crescendo each time, and their voices only repeated those words with stronger purpose. My piano playing was anointed as God led me in creative ways to embellish the song and convey its emotion through my hands at the keyboard. I saw groups of four and five men and women joining arms on shoulders or raising arms joined at the hands. Every bit of it was spontaneous in response to their love for the Lord---such a beautiful yet commanding presence.

We are all creations of God, but when we put our faith in Jesus, in that moment we are given the right to be called children of God and become a part of the family of God.

> *In the beginning was the Word, and the Word was with God, and the Word was God. He was with God in the beginning. Through him all things were made; without him nothing was made that*

has been made. In him was life, and that life was the light of all mankind. The light shines in the darkness, and the darkness has not overcome it. There was a man sent from God whose name was John. He came as a witness to testify concerning that light, so that through him all might believe. He himself was not the light; he came only as a witness to the light. The true light that gives light to everyone was coming into the world. He was in the world, and though the world was made through him, the world did not recognize him. He came to that which was his own, but his own did not receive him. Yet to **all who did receive him, to those who believed in his name, he gave the right to become children of God**—*children born not of natural descent, nor of human decision or a husband's will, but born of God. The Word became flesh and made his dwelling among us. We have seen his glory, the glory of the one and only Son, who came from the Father, full of grace and truth. For the law was given through Moses; grace and truth came through Jesus Christ. (John 1:1–14, 17 NIV, emphasis mine)*

*See what great love the Father has lavished on us, that we should be called **children of God**! And that is what we are!* **The reason the world does not know us is that it did not know him**. *(I John 3:1 NIV, emphasis mine)*

*So in Christ Jesus you are all **children of God through faith**, for all of you who were baptized into Christ have clothed yourselves with Christ. There is neither Jew nor Gentile, neither slave nor free, nor is there male and female, for you are all one in Christ Jesus.* ***If you belong to Christ***, *then you are Abraham's seed, and heirs according to the promise. (Galatians 3:26–29 NIV, emphasis mine)*

Sometimes we have to stand alone for what is right, but we must never forget that Jesus promised in the latter part of Matthew 28:20 (NASB), "...and lo, I am with you always, even to the end of the age." Come not alone because we have:

- a family headed by Creator God the Father and joined by Jesus Christ, the Son, who secured our adoption with His blood;
- the Holy Spirit, who took up residence in our hearts so that we are never alone; and
- people of faith around the world who share our struggles, celebrate common victories, regroup after failures, and emerge victorious for the Kingdom of God.

Come not alone because God sees you individually, and His view is not of an insignificant pile of dust fashioned into a human being fraught with frailty and failures. What He sees is His finest creation with all of His unique finishing touches, a child so valuable He could not bear to be separated from His creation by sin, of which He can have no part and remain righteous. After considering all the options at His disposal for saving this extraordinary creation, He made the only choice that would correct the course for all eternity because the correction required a sinless sacrifice tortured and shredded.

Sin is hated that bad by God, and there are centuries of it and wrongs because of it to be avenged. It is no wonder a few drops of blood sprinkled here and there would not suffice to appease God's wrath. God required every drop of blood, every slice of skin, each dissected sinew, each pounding of the fist, all the hatred, all the anger, the separation, the betrayal, and loneliness heaped on Jesus. Because God loved each person completely—leaving nothing any of us could do to make God love us more or love us less—God sent His only begotten Son into our world, taking on human flesh to experience all the trials and temptations and to become our sacrificial lamb, so that whosoever believes in Jesus would not perish but have everlasting life with Him.

Our Heavenly Father offered and still offers salvation through Jesus Christ to all human beings, regardless of the severity of sins committed, so they do not have to go to hell in payment of those sins. He respects humans enough to make the options clear and allow them to make the choice. God's "wants," however, depended on Jesus' willingness to cooperate and ability to endure all the way through death, burial, and resurrection. Jesus loved the world so much that He laid down His life as a ransom for many.

> *It is not that God hates unbelievers so much He sends them to hell, but rather, He loves them so much He sent Jesus to the cross.*
> **Micah Duckett**

As we close, hear God speak to you by name in His words from Psalm 139, printed first as it appears in Scripture, and then personalized for you:

> *You have searched me, LORD, and you know me. You know when I sit and when I rise; you perceive my thoughts from afar. You discern my going out and my lying down; you are familiar with all my ways. Before a word is on my tongue you, LORD, know it completely. You hem me in behind and before, and you lay your hand upon me. Such knowledge is too wonderful for me, too lofty for me to attain. Where can I go from your Spirit? Where can I flee from your presence? If I go up to the heavens, you are there; if I make my bed in the depths, you are there. If I rise on the wings of the dawn, if I settle on the far side of the sea, even there your hand will guide me, your right hand will hold me fast. If I say, "Surely the darkness will hide me and the light become night around me," even the darkness will not be dark to you; the night will shine like the day, for darkness is as light to you. For you created my inmost being; you knit me together in my mother's womb. I praise you because I am fearfully and wonderfully made; your works are wonderful, I know that full well. My frame was not hidden from you when I was*

made in the secret place, when I was woven together in the depths of the earth. Your eyes saw my unformed body; all the days ordained for me were written in your book before one of them came to be. How precious to me are your thoughts, God! How vast is the sum of them! Were I to count them, they would outnumber the grains of sand— when I awake, I am still with you. (Psalm 139:1–18 NIV)

Now read and be encouraged from the passage personalized as from God to you:

I have searched you and known you. I the Lord know when you sit and when you rise; I perceive your thoughts from afar. I discern your going out and your lying down; I am familiar with all your ways. Before a word is on your tongue, I the Lord know it completely. I hem you in behind and before, and I lay My hand upon you. Such knowledge seems too wonderful for you, too lofty to attain. Where can you go from My Spirit? Where can you flee from My presence? If you go up to the heavens, I am there; if you make your bed in the depths, I am there. If you rise on the wings of the dawn, if you settle on the far side of the sea, even there MY hand will guide YOU, MY right hand will hold you fast. If you say, "Surely the darkness will hide me and the light become night around me," even the darkness will not be dark to ME; the night will shine like the day, for darkness is as light to Me. For I the Lord created your inmost being; I am the One who knit you together in your mother's womb. I hear you praise Me because you are fearfully and wonderfully made; My works are indeed wonderful, and you know that full well. Your frame was not hidden from Me when you were made in the secret place, when I the Lord wove you together in the depths of the earth. My eyes saw your unformed body; all the days ordained for you were written in My book before one of them came to be (before conception). How precious are My thoughts of you and how vast is the sum of them! Were you to count them, they would outnumber the grains of sand— when you awake, you are still with Me and I with you. (Psalm 139:1–18 personalized)

Reader's Guide for Group Discussion or Self Study

Chapter 1: Not Prepared
1. What did you take away from chapter one?
2. Share your "not prepared" experience, current or past. What was your emergency response?
3. Were you able to trace God's hand at work on your behalf? If not, how did faith play a role?
4. What did God teach you about Himself in the process?
5. How has God used your experience to encourage another person?

Chapter 2: Not with the Perfect Ending
1. Did chapter two help you come to terms with not having all the answers to the hard questions of life? Was any part especially meaningful to you?
2. Share your story of tragic loss or a loved one's experience with it that touched your heart.
3. How did it impact your life? How did it influence your relationship with God and those around you?
4. How do you feel about God not intervening to give you a better outcome?
5. What questions do you have for God? Spend time individually, in pairs, or as a group praying for God's

peace, patience, and provision as He writes the rest of your story.

Chapter 3: Not Like I Imagined

1. What is your shattered dream story?
2. Did it change your perspective of God? If so, in what way?
3. Was your faith impacted?
4. Have you figured out how God had a guiding hand in your journey? Can you see how God can take the pieces of your shattered dream, which are impossible for human hands to repurpose, and work those shards for good? If not, how do you handle not having all the answers you seek?
5. Did you identify with what it is like to form a misconception in childhood that you realize as an adult was not like you imagined?
6. Do you need God to do a miracle in your heart in order to move forward and/or help with healing? If you have a willing spirit to receive healing, wait until eternity to get all your answers, and move forward by faith in the meantime, then have a seat in the middle of the group and allow them to lay hands on and pray for you. If you are using this guide on your own, lay your hands one on top of the other on your heart, and empty your soul's cries to God. He can act on your behalf with or without a group.

Chapter 4: Not Knowing What Will Happen

1. Have you experienced what it is like to be in financial need? If so, was the problem of your own making, or were you thrust into it through no fault of your own?

2. Have you had a time where you needed a different type of provision from God but had no clue how things would turn out? Share your experience.
3. How did the situation impact your family or you?
4. How did your journey affect your faith? What did you learn about the mettle of God's character and care?
5. What needs of others has God brought to your attention without them necessarily asking you for assistance? Pray for discernment about how God might want to use you as His mouth, arms, hands, feet and/or pocketbook. Perhaps it could be a group, family, or solo ministry project that you do anonymously.

Chapter 5: Not What I Wanted

1. How did God speak to you through chapter five?
2. Have you, a friend or a loved one been impacted by a health crisis or disability?
3. Have you had a new normal thrust on you that you did not request or want? How are you handling it? Share your story.
4. Has God showed you a new purpose to go with your new normal? Give an example of how He has used you.
5. How has God enabled you to move forward, or are you still struggling with that? Take a moment to ask God to inspire you to be all He wants you to be in your new normal while you give Him time to heal you either here on earth or in heaven.

Chapter 6: Not Getting It Right

1. Can you identify with looking for open doors and signs from God to point you toward His will for your life or for a decision you need to make?

2. Share an example of how that did or did not work out for you.
3. In the moments when your good intentions led you to a mistake, how did God respond? Did He intervene to rescue you right away or did He let you struggle to teach you something?
4. What did you learn from chapter six about how easy it is to end up following signs or people instead of following God?
5. Are you afraid to get honest with God about the mess(es) you have made? Do you fear rejection if you approach Him? Were you able to take away something from chapter six to help you come boldly to God with full assurance that He knew about your mistakes before you did and He would rather come to your aid than cut you loose?

Chapter 7: Not Accepted
1. What makes a person feel not accepted? Have you been guilty of not being as inclusive as you could have been?
2. Have you been hurt, verbally accosted, or otherwise disillusioned by "church people?" Without exposing names, briefly share how that came about.
3. Did it cause you to walk away from church and/or God for a time? Are you still in that place, and if so, what did you take away from chapter seven that might aid in your return? If we attend church to worship and express our love for the Lord, why would we allow the actions and words of others cut us off from that?
4. Have you considered that God accepts you and proved His love for you at Calvary? What did you learn from chapter 7 about your value to God?

5. When has God called in His "cavalry" to confirm, strengthen, and establish you during a spiritual attack? Have you ever been a part of the cavalry?

Chapter 8: Not Strong Enough
1. Do you believe in spiritual warfare? If so, share a time when you knew you were under spiritual attack.
2. Are you feeling the blows of spiritual attack today? Do you find it difficult to climb your way out of the pit? Did you feel like the prayer at the end of the chapter was written for you?
3. Have you considered fighting from a kneeling stance through prayer and partnering with someone to pray for you? Take a moment to pray for any needs expressed in this regard.
4. When have you been guilty of being the spiritual attacker, whether the recipient knew it was happening or was out of earshot? Dare to be candid.
5. Brainstorm some ways you can splash encouragement on those in leadership roles.

Chapter 9: Not in a Good Place
1. Describe your "not good" place. It could be that your mind is not in a good place right now because of problems…your home is not a good place…a relationship is not in a good place, etc.
2. How are you handling it? How are you bringing God's salt and light into the situation?
3. Are you the cause of the "not good" place? What can you do to change that?
4. Share a time when God helped you remedy your "not good" place.

5. Spend time asking God as applicable to change your situation or change you, change the other person or change you, etc.

Chapter 10: Not Feeling God's Love
1. Describe a time when you questioned if God cared about what was happening in your life or a loved one's life. What made you question it?
2. Have you ever felt unloved by God? Why? Did your feelings hamper you from praying or drawing close to God?
3. Have you considered that God wants you to come to Him, even if you're mad at Him, doubting His care, or questioning His existence?
4. If you are convinced or almost convinced that God cannot possibly love you if He allowed your circumstances, have you stopped to consider that Satan might have you deceived about God's love? What did you take away from chapter ten about Satan's tactics vs. Calvary's proof of God's love?
5. Share a time when a speck of faith blossomed into life changing spiritual growth.

Chapter 11: Not Able to Let it Go
1. What is the hardest thing you've had to forgive? Were you the hero of your story, and if so, what did that feel like afterward?
2. If you still struggle with unforgiveness, did God speak to you through chapter eleven and empower you to move forward with forgiving, even if the offender is no longer living?

3. When have you been the one that needs to be forgiven? Are you remorseful? Do you need to forgive yourself, or do you need the forgiveness from another person? Both?
4. How does forgiveness prevent bad behavior from destroying our hearts?
5. Talk about things God has to forgive where people are concerned, and don't give the "pat" Sunday School answers. Dig deeper with your responses. Then spend time in private prayer comparing what God forgives to what you are asked to forgive. Think about whose list is harder to forgive. Be brave enough to let God speak to you with raw honesty. This could be a shackle-freeing moment of obedience to God and worship experience for some of you.

Chapter 12: Not Recognizing God's Voice

1. How do you "know that you know that you know" when God is speaking to you? Share a time when you sensed God telling you to do something and how you responded or failed to respond.
2. How would you feel if you attempted to deliver an important message but the recipient ignored you and made no attempt to hear you? Have you ever stopped to consider that God wants to be noticed and heard? How do you think God feels when He is not noticed or heard?
3. When you are in a relationship with another person, how would it be impacted if one of you did all the giving and the other did all the taking? Would it bother you if the other person only had time for you when something was needed? How are you impacted when

you consider that God is always there for you, even when you haven't been as attentive to your relationship as you should have been?
4. When have you been on the receiving end of the blessing because someone was obedient to respond to God's instruction to help you or bless you in some way? When were you the anonymous blesser?
5. What can a person do to be more aware of God's promptings?

Epilogue: Not Alone
1. Share a time when you felt like you were standing alone for your faith or a spiritual principle?
2. How can you hold to a conviction and speak truth if necessary without crossing the line on judging or condemning in social circles, the workplace, social media, etc.? How does Satan bait you into looking more like the world with your attitude or message delivery than being salt and light?
3. Why do you think the Lord mentions so often things like the following: He is with you always, He will never leave you or forsake you, He is a friend that sticks closer than a brother, nothing shall ever separate you from the love of God, etc.? Pause to meditate on Him speaking these things to you directly…one on one. Substitute your name in the blanks: God is with _____ always; God will never leave _____ or forsake _____; God is a friend who sticks closer than a brother to _____; nothing shall ever separate _____ from the love of God.
4. Why is it important to support fellow Christians, even when your denominations and doctrines may differ?

How are we connected? Keeping in mind battle tactics, why would Satan try to separate us and even make us turn on one another?

5. Here is a popular debate topic, "Will God send people to hell who have never had the opportunity to hear the gospel or the name of Jesus, or who sincerely tried to find their way to God but picked a path other than Jesus?" The answer to this might depend for starters on how you process what God says on the subject and if you hold that the problem to overcome is a hearing problem (i.e., people have to hear the gospel some way; if they don't hear, they cannot be held responsible; etc.)

   a. Could the problem be that they rejected what they have heard and what God made evident about Himself and divine nature? If a person truly desires to know God, will they be able to find Him without human assistance to the right path? What insight do you get from Romans 1:20–32, Romans 3:11, and Deuteronomy 4:29?

   b. If upon death God would indeed grant mercy to a person who never heard of Jesus or was trying to sincerely find Him but followed a path other than Jesus, then would it be better if we never told anyone about Jesus so they could remain innocently ignorant and not run the risk of going to hell? Is there any Scripture that would support this? I could not find one.

   c. Instead I found many passages on the urgency or need to tell others the gospel of Jesus Christ. Let's look at a few. How do John 3:1–19, Matthew 28:19–20, John 14:6, Luke 10:2, John 10:9, and Acts 1:8 shed light on the urgency of the command to spread the gospel because people will be sent to hell without Jesus? What is the urgency if not for this reason?

d. What part does faith play in leaving it up to God to be responsible for a fair and equitable opportunity to be given to every human to be presented with the gospel, even if He does not use humans as His mouthpiece nor reveals to us the mystery of how He delivers the gospel without a human being as the messenger?

e. If there were many paths leading to God, why would Jesus leave heaven and go through the torture of the cross? What is required by God to atone for sin?

6. What are your insights on Psalm 139, and how can this passage be useful to you during the times you feel alone in the battles of your life? Did the personalized version of Psalm 139 leave you with any impressions?

Study Notes and Journal

Study Notes and Journal

Study Notes and Journal

Study Notes and Journal

Study Notes and Journal

Study Notes and Journal

Study Notes and Journal

Study Notes and Journal

Study Notes and Journal

Made in the USA
Middletown, DE
07 August 2017